HOW TO MASTER THE ART OF FINISHING

Jim Chatterton

Copyright @ 2022 Jim Chatterton

This book was first published in 2016 by JIM CHATTERTON

The moral right of Jim Chatterton to be identified as the author of this work has been asserted by him in accordance with the Copyright, Designs and Patents act 1988.

All rights reserved. No part of this publication may be reproduced, distributed or transmitted in any form or by any means, including photocopying, recording, or other electronic or mechanical methods, without the prior written permission of the author, except in the case of brief quotations embodied in critical reviews and certain other non-commercial uses permitted by copyright law

Copyright @ 2016 @ 2017 @2022

Cover Design: Jim Chatterton

Copyright © Jim Chatterton

"Scoring for show, Doubles for dough"

—Bobby George...

Foreword

This book is part of a four-book series that are designed to give any darts player a complete and thorough education in the art of finishing. If there was ever a university course that specialized in darts finishing, the four books in this series are what they would be teaching.

Each book covers a different area, and they all combine to give the most thorough explanation of finishing ever attempted.

This is the core book of the series, and it focuses on the finishes from 2-170. Every finish is looked at in great detail, and different ways of approaching them are discussed, depending on the situations you find yourself in. If there was just one book that every darts player should have in their possession, this is the one they should have.

Knowing the out-shot combinations – *I mean really knowing them* – is a skill set that every darts player should strive to master. And yet very few ever do.

By following an extremely powerful, and yet easy to use step-by step system, this book takes years off the learning curve and shows you how to develop a World Class level of finishing – no matter where you are currently at.

Here are some of the key points this book covers:

- **Know every finish from 2-170**
- **Never again stop to work out what you need midway through your throw**
- **Instinctively know what to throw for every time, regardless of the situation**
- **Know different, effective strategies for finishing, depending on the situation**

- Gain a massive advantage over your opponents
- Use a simple yet powerful 3-step process that leads to the Holy Grail of
- Darts Finishing – **MATHEMATICAL ENLIGHTENMENT** that removes the need for mathematics once and for all

All this and much, much more.

If you are a player that has aspirations of regularly reaching the latter stages of tournaments, and becoming the best player you can possibly become, then this book is for you. Tournaments are won and lost on fine margins, and possessing a thorough knowledge of the complete art of finishing may be the difference between winning the tournament and losing in one of the early rounds. That's how important it is.

The information in this book gives a complete and thorough education on everything you will ever need to know about the art of finishing. Master these and you will be a very formidable player, capable of competing with the very best.

For more information about the other books in this series go to www.DartsFinishing.com. They are also shown at the back of this book. Make sure you get them and study them. The priceless information they contain will knock years off your learning curve and will remain with you for the remainder of your playing career.

I wish you the very best of luck in your darting career as you move up the ladder of success…….

Jim Chatterton

Contents

Foreword iv

Introduction 1

How to use this book 5

Chapter One: 2 to 40 13

Chapter Two: 41-60 35

Chapter Three: 61-80 45

Chapter Four: 81-90 63

Chapter Five: 91-95 75

Chapter Six: 96-100 87

Chapter Seven: 101-120 95

Chapter Eight: 121-130 111

Chapter Nine: 131-140 123

Chapter Ten: 141-150 135

Chapter Eleven: 151-160 153

Chapter Twelve: 161-170 167

Conclusion 179

Bonus Chapter – Finishing Routines and Practice Games 181

Appendix 199

About the Author 219

Other Books in this series: 220

Other Books in this series: 221

Other Books in this series: 222

Introduction

How many times have you watched a player fly down the dartboard and get so far ahead it looks impossible for him or her to lose, only to see them mess up the finish and lose the game or stop with a blank stare as they do not know what to throw at?

This happens every night of the week all over the world and is probably the number one cause of frustration in the game of darts. Knowing the out-shot combinations –*I mean really knowing them* – is a skill set that every dart player should strive to master, and yet very few ever do. There is no greater feeling in darts - other than winning the event - than hitting a 100+ finish when your opponent is sat on a one or two dart out, and if you follow the methods described in this book you will be the player who is able to consistently hit the big out-shots when needed.

I have defined and devised a step-by-step process that will quickly and easily take any player from knowing nothing about darts finishing, to mastering the subtle art in as short amount of time as possible.

This book, if studied carefully and diligently, will knock years off the learning curve. The only constraints are the amount of time and effort you put into learning the material presented here.

We have all seen players that seemingly know every out-shot combination easily and effortlessly, and this is certainly true at the higher levels of play, but even the experts had to start somewhere. Practicing the doubles and knowing the finishing combinations should be the number one priority of any practice session. Sure, throwing at the treble 20 and trying to hit the 180's makes you feel good about your game, but it is the player who diligently and regularly practices his or her doubles and finishes that usually ends up being the better player and winning the important matches.

If you play 501 at any level competitively, knowing your out-shot combinations is the most important skill to learn. Knowing instinctively what to go for every time you step up to the board, no matter what number you are left with is a huge advantage over the player that aimlessly throws at the treble 20 hoping to leave himself somewhere near a double.

Equally important is the skill to immediately know what to do if one of your darts misses its intended target. Instead of stopping to work it out or asking the marker what is left (and then having to work out what to go for once he's told you), this book explains in clear detail how to systematically and easily learn every combination you will ever need to know to become a player everyone respects and fears for their finishing prowess.

Any player will tell you that the players they fear the most are the ones who are able to finish quickly and easily. No matter how superior they may feel they are at the scoring phase, these players are always worried about the ones who can hit the doubles when it counts, especially the ones who seem to know every combination like the back of their hands. This book will take you to that level.

You will learn what to go for if the number you are needing is blocked by another dart, or if you need two of the same number and the first dart is only just sticking in the board and one more thrown at it may knock it out.

If you already possess advanced knowledge of all the finishes, then I congratulate you, as you are in the 1% of players at this level. This book can still be of help to you as it may give you some other options if your preferred route is not working on any given day. In short, this book will help anyone who wants to join the 1% of players that possess the massive advantage of knowing every finish from 2 to 170 without missing a beat.

If used as described, the methods detailed within these pages will take any player from not knowing anything about finishing to a level where mathematics no longer come into the equation. You will instinctively know what to throw for under any situation and for any combination that you may require. This gives a player such a huge advantage and is one of the key components to taking a player where he or she wants to go within the game of darts.

As long as you use a standard dartboard as shown below then everything in this book applies to you. I make only the assumptions that you already have a set of darts, have access to a dartboard for practice, and that you are able, at first, to be able to do simple subtractions. Once you get into the principles of what I am about to show you then you will no longer need to do simple subtractions.

To avoid any confusion, here is a picture of a standard dartboard that you need to play the game of 501:

The finishes are broken down into bite sized groups in order of difficulty and importance. Each chapter builds onto the next and as you will discover, patterns emerge that once learned, will stay with you forever.

Like anything else in life, you will only get out of this book what you put into it. While learning the finishes is easy (and if you don't believe me now you will by the time you reach the end), being able to hit them consistently in any situation requires dedication and practice. Whatever your aspirations are in this wonderful game that has brought pleasure to millions of people around the world, I wish you all the very best of luck as we unravel the mysteries of the dartboard together.

Jim Chatterton

How to use this book

The information contained in the following chapters are laid out in an easy to use system that builds upon itself in such a way that by the time the reader reaches the end of the book he or she will have a complete encyclopedic knowledge of every finish from 2 to 170 and in many cases, will have several different options for each finish at their disposal.

In the appendix at the end of the book, there is a chapter on practice routines designed especially for finishing. By utilizing these routines in your regular practice sessions, you will see massive advances in both your confidence and skill. Once you are hitting the finishes regularly in practice, you will begin to expect to hit them in match-play situations, and this is when you become a very dangerous adversary.

By rotating the routines in the appendix, you will avoid the boredom that inevitably arises when you throw for the same thing over and over. The routines contained in the appendices are fluid and ever changing, and they will test you to the limits of your abilities.

With the exception of the warm-up routine, all the routines are designed to replicate the tensions and feelings you get in regular match-play. Not only will this be a huge aid when it comes to real life match-play, it also forces you to try 100% with each and every dart, and this is huge. This is the reason your skill and confidence will blast through the roof in the shortest amount of time.

I have devised and developed a 3-step method of mastering the finishes that is easy to understand, easy to learn, and applies to every single finish from the bottom to the top. Mastering the 3 steps to finishing leads you naturally and easily to the 4th and final step – **Mathematical Enlightenment.**

Mathematical Enlightenment is achieved when you instinctively know every finish you are left with – without any math involved. Whatever you need, you automatically and easily know the solution. Reach this level – and it is nowhere near as difficult as you may think if you follow the methods in this book – and you will truly master the dartboard.

Commit yourself to learning these methods, and put in the required effort to do it. This is a one-time learning experience that will benefit you for the remainder of your playing career. This is as big of a win-win situation as you will ever encounter in darts, as it lays out the details before you. So, commit yourself to studying and learning this method. It will reward you for the rest of your life.

So, what are these step-by-step methods? Don't be fooled by their simplicity. Together they create a logical and powerful path to finishing freedom and mastery, and once applied and learned, will become second nature:

The Step-By-Step process that you should learn by heart and commit to memory:

1. Always know what you have left before throwing your darts
2. Is your opponent on a finish? Yes, or No.
3. Knowing the answers to steps 1 and 2, always know how to finish the number you are currently left on.

Let's break this down some more:

Step 1

Always know what you have left before throwing your darts

Before stepping up to the board to take your shot, you should ALWAYS know what score you have left. Steps 2 and 3 will dictate how you go for the shot, but the first thing you should know is what you need to hit in order to finish the game.

After each dart is thrown, always know what you have left. You will never be able to master the art of finishing if you don't know for sure what it is you are throwing at.

At first, you may have to stop after throwing a dart to work out what is left before continuing. This is why you practice alone, somewhere you can be undisturbed and can concentrate fully on learning the different combinations.

Step 2

Is your opponent on a finish? Yes, or No

The 2nd question can be answered quickly and easily before you step up to the board to take your shot. A quick glance at the scoreboard tells you everything you need to know, and is a simple yes or no answer.

Never assume that your opponent will not hit the finish he or she is sitting on. Even if it is 143, or some other unlikely finish, always assume they are going to get it. Many darts matches are lost because of opponents being underestimated. If you have a shot at taking it out when they are on a finish, do so. Let them worry about you, not the other way around.

Step 3
Knowing the answers to steps 1 and 2, always know how to finish the number you are currently left on.

Step 3 is where this book is concentrated. By the time you have finished it, you will know exactly what to throw for in any set of circumstances.

Shot selection is greatly affected depending on whether you have 2 or 3 darts in your hands, along with the answer to question 2. There are a couple of basic rules of step 3 that must never be broken:

If your opponent is on a finish, always try to take out the finish you are on with the darts that are in your hands. It is far better to go out on your shield by throwing for a shot and missing, than it is setting yourself up for the next turn. That next turn will probably never happen, so commit to the finish and go for it.

Never throw at the bullseye when you have 50 remaining when you have more than 1 dart in your hands. The bullseye is the smallest target on the board and the most difficult to hit. You always throw at the shot offering the greatest percentage odds. The outer ring doubles are a much bigger target than the bullseye, and should be used whenever possible to give you a greater chance of success.

Sure, you may hit it, and it looks great when you do. But you are playing Russian roulette with the board, and you will lose more often than you win. You may get lucky and land in an even single big enough to leave a double, but more likely you will land in an odd number, or the outer bull ring. Then all you can do is setup the shot for when you return the next time. There will probably not be a next time, so don't do it.

3 step process in action:

You stand behind your opponent while he is taking his turn on the dartboard. While he is throwing, you look to see what score you have remaining. You are left on 67. This is step 1.

Once your opponent has finished his turn, you look to see what he has left before you step up to throw. He requires 42. Step 2 asks one simple question – is your opponent on a finish – yes or no? In this example the answer is obviously yes, so this answers step 2.

Now step 3 comes into action. Because you studied this book, you know how to finish the number you are left on – in this example it is 67.

So, you walk up to the oche and throw the first dart at T17 to leave D8. It misses the treble and lands in the single 17. This is where all 3 steps combine, which is why it is a very powerful method that works every time.

Because you know how to finish 67 with all the options available to you, your knowledge answers steps 1 and 3 simultaneously. Step 2 doesn't change while you are at the oche. Because you hit the single 17, you now require 50, which will leave a single 18, D16; a 10, D20; or even 14, D18, whichever is your preference.

The shot changes dramatically if you have 2 darts left in your hands:

You require 67, step 1 checked.

Your opponent is on 42. Yes, he/she is on a finish. Step 2 checked.

You have 2 darts in your hands and you have to try to take out the shot on this turn. Because you know every scenario you will ever need with the finish of 67, you know that you will throw for T17 with the first dart, trying to leave yourself on D8 with the last dart. You also know that if you hit the single 17, you will leave yourself on 50 with 1 dart remaining

If you repeat the above 3 steps every time you step up to the board, it will quickly become second nature and you will be doing it without even thinking about it. If you apply step 3 to every finish in this book, *in the linear order they are presented*, the numbers cease to be mathematical, and instead they become an extension of the dartboard. 67 is no longer just a number, it is now T17, D8, or single 17, 18, D16 etc. This is when you have reached step 4 – Mathematical Enlightenment.

Learning the finishes

The finishes build upon each other in a logical manner. By learning them one by one in sequence, you are guaranteeing that whatever you hit with the dart currently in your hand, you will immediately know how to get whatever number you leave, and this is the key.

By starting at the very beginning, you take all the guesswork out of what you have left when the dart in your hand misses its intended target. You apply step 1, readjust, and throw for the correct numbers. You keep your rhythm, you keep your momentum, and you retain your accuracy. Every time! Because learning the finishes one by one is so important, it is recommended that this is done solo. You will be amazed at how quickly you will get these down.

Once you learn the finishes from 2-60, you will have learnt a huge percentage of the finishes you will ever find yourself on. Learn them from 2-80 and you will know around 90% of every finish you will ever need. Most of the bigger, 100+ finishes are just a smaller one with a big treble added to it.

Things you need to know

For clarity, I will interchange the terms he or she when referring to a player but please know that everything contained within these pages applies to all genders and all age groups.

Each chapter builds on the knowledge from the previous chapter, so make sure you have a thorough grasp of everything before moving on to the next. To make it easier, I have included exercises in each chapter to help nail it down and "get it in your head."

This book is hands on and is designed to be learned by doing rather than sitting and reading. If you only read this and don't practice what is taught, then you are only getting around 40% of the potential within the pages. By reading and understanding the reasons why we go for a finish in a certain way, then investing the time to practice the exercises until they are firmly embedded into your brain and your fingers you will not only get everything out of the book that you possibly can; you will also reach the point where mathematics is no longer required.

By repetitively practicing the exercises you will also get the muscle memory required to be able to hit any double on the dartboard, and it is when you reach this point that you will become the formidable player you want to be.

At the beginning of each chapter there is a table with all the finishes to focus on. Once you have looked over them and read them it is time to begin practicing them and getting them into your brain, one at a time.

Next, practice them all in sequence. Learn the other options as they are presented. Find the ones that are best suited to your own game and practice these as much as possible until you know them inside out. Be aware of the other options, but use the ones that you like the best. This is the core of the book and is the most important section to master.

It is always preferable to leave a double that splits down easily in even numbers, such as double 16. It is for this very reason that double 16 is the preferred double to leave by the vast majority of players. It breaks down to 16, 8, 4 and 2 which give the best possible chance of success without having to split an odd number.

However, don't become a slave to double 16. By this, I mean don't fall into the trap of leaving it at the expense of more appropriate finishes that may be available. If you follow the guidelines presented here, you will know when and when not to leave certain favored doubles.

Left-handed players tend to favor the right-hand side of the dartboard more than right handed players who tend to favor the left-hand side of the board more. For this reason, I have included many finishes that are more acceptable to left-handers, with most of them ending on double 20 and double 10. However, this will come down to personal preference.

To make sure that you have reached the required level of knowledge before moving onto the next chapter, I have included a series of 10 questions at the end of each chapter. If you have to stop and think to answer any of them, please go back and make sure you know it thoroughly – without the need to think about it – before moving on.

Abbreviations used in this book

T = Treble

D = Double

S = Single

B = Bullseye (Red 50)

O/B = Outer Bull (Green 25)

Chapter One: 2 to 40

Most players will look at the chapter heading and think they can skip it and move to chapter 2. After all, these are the easy ones that everyone knows, right? Hopefully by the time you reach the end of the chapter you will understand that even the easiest of finishes are more complex than first imagined. By learning the methods with a higher percentage chance of success you will be laying strong foundations that will be built upon as the book progresses. It takes all the guesswork out of the equation. Once studied and learned properly, the finishes will be automatic and more of a reflex action.

Unless you are already an accomplished player I implore you not to ignore this very important chapter. The finishes in this category are the most important finishes you will ever work on as they will represent every double you will ever hit outside of the bullseye.

It is easier to learn the finishes by actually doing it on the dartboard and not just reading it, although this helps as well, especially at first when you begin to learn them. This is the method adopted all the way through this book.

Here are the finishes you will be working on in this chapter:

Number	Solution
2	D1
3	1, D1
4	D2
5	1, D2 3, D1
6	D3 2, D2
7	3, D2
8	D4
9	1, D4
10	D5 2, D4
11	3, D4
12	D6 4, D4
13	5, D4

14	D7 6, D4
15	7, D4 3, D6
16	D8
17	1, D8 9, D4
18	D9 2, D8
19	3, D8 11, D4
20	D10
21	5, D8 13, D4 1, D10
22	D11 6, D8 2, D10
23	7, D8 3, D10
24	D12 8, D8

	4, D10
25	9, D8 17, D4 1, D12 5, D10
26	D13 10, D8 2, D12 6, D10
27	11, D8 3, D12 19, D4 7, D10
28	D14 12, D8 4, D12 8, D10
29	13, D8 5, D12 9, D10
30	D15 14, D8 6, D12 10, D10
31	15, D8

	7, D12 11, D10
32	D16
33	1, D16 17, D8 9, D12 13, D10
34	D17 2, D16 10, D12 14, D10
35	3, D16 19, D8 11, D12 15, D10
36	D18
37	5, D16 1, D18 13, D12 17, D10
38	D19 6, D16 2, D18 14, D12 18, D10

39	7, D16 3, D18 15, D12 19, D10
40	D20

At first glance, this may look like an overcomplicated view of what is a simple area of finishing. It is always good to have options, and it is from knowing all your options that you will find your favorite ways to finish and make good decisions.

The big dilemma is always related to unusual doubles. Let's say you are left with 38 and you have all 3 darts in your hand. Do you go straight for it, or do you break it down to leave a better double? There is no set precedence with this, and as always it comes down to how you feel about it at that particular moment. If you feel confident then go for it. If not, then split it. If you are on 38 and only have 2 or even one dart in your hand, then I would always recommend going straight for it. It is always better to throw for a finish and miss than to set up a better double and never have a chance to hit it.

Practice

Now it is time to set aside some time and practice these finishes until they become automatic and you can hit them without even thinking. It takes time, but it is time well spent as you move up to the more involved finishes in the following chapters.

Starting at the first finish in the table (double 1); spend some time on each one. If applicable, choose the option that is best suited to your own game, and practice them one at a time as you ingrain them into your brain.

Take note of what numbers are left when your darts miss their intended targets. If you practice these enough, you will quickly and easily learn what all the possible combinations are, and you won't have to stop and think about it when you miss.

Don't move onto the next one until you know the current finish very well without referring to the charts. This way, you will know every finish below the one you are currently learning. It won't matter what you leave yourself on at this point because you will know every finish below it.

Practice Sessions

Always set aside a small amount of time to warm up rather than diving straight into a practice session. This allows your arm to get into the groove and iron out any stiffness or kinks in your throw before beginning the serious practice. A good way to warm up is by throwing at the bull. Once you start to hit it with some regularity then it is time to move on to the main focus of your practice.

If you are a newer player and still find hitting the bulls difficult, don't stress over it and aim for just one dart in the bull and move up from there as your skill and confidence grows. Whatever you decide to do for a warm up, it shouldn't last more than 5 or 10 minutes.

As this is a book all about finishing, and as we all know that finishing is the most important part of the game of 501, it makes sense that you practice hitting doubles! The trebles and scoring can be practiced in another session (although when you reach the higher finishes you get plenty of practice at the trebles).

You are now going to hit every double twice, but with a twist. You could just go around the board from 1 to 20, hit the bull and come back to 1, and that would work just fine. However, you are practicing for the game of 501 (or any 01 game), so it makes sense to practice with this in mind.

Rather than go around the board linearly, you are going to start at D20, and then throw as you would in a proper game. Therefore, if you throw at D20 and hit a single 20, next you throw at D10, and then D5. This gets you used to throwing the same way as you would in a match-play environment and gives you an edge because you are always used to throwing at doubles in the same manor.

So, you get to D5, then what? Well, then you have gotten as far as you can get in this segment, so you come back up again. You hit D5, D10, and then D20. You always go as far as the breakdown of that number allows before coming back up again.

Next you move onto D19. As this does not break down you hit it twice (it doesn't have to be in the same throw although that's always nice to do). Then it is the turn of the 18's, and you hit D18, D9, D9 and then D18 again. This may look complicated at first, but it is easy once you have done it a time or two,.

Continue in this manor until you reach D11. Again, you hit two of those and then the outer ring of doubles is done. It is now time for the bullseye, and this time you have to hit two of the red, center bulls. The red bull is double the green ring (25 points), and is the highest double you can finish on. It is also the most difficult, and it comes into play a lot more as you get into the higher finishing combinations as you will see.

For clarity, the doubles warm up routine is shown in the table below. If time allows, always complete this before moving onto the actual finishes. The more you can practice hitting the doubles the better you will be when it comes to the real thing.

20	10	5	5	10	20				
19	19								
18	9	9	18						
17	17								
16	8	4	2	1	1	2	4	8	16
15	15								
14	7								
13	13								
12	6	3	3	6	12				
11	11								
B	B								

At first this may take a while to complete, but don't give up. Mastering the art of finishing is as difficult as it gets in the game of darts, and the more you practice the easier it will get. As a rough guide, eventually the entire sequence detailed above will take you no more than 15-20 minutes once you reach a good level. If you can do it faster than that then you are a very formidable player indeed!

If you are short on time, or if you are a new player, doing the entire routine may not be a good option for you. In this case, hit just one of each double rather than two.

Although this is a good practice routine in itself, it won't teach you how to finish. So, make sure you spend the bulk of your available time learning the finishes as explained in detail below.

Practice routine

At this stage you are going to cycle through the finishes in the 2 to 40 range as many times as it takes to get these finishes firmly in your brain. It may look easy on paper, but this is the foundation for everything else that follows and is vital that you don't skip over this very important step.

Going off the chart at the beginning of this chapter; cycle through all the finishes from 2-40. Try each of the different combinations and pick out the ones that you like the best as your preferred options.

Most players prefer D16 as their preferred double, and this makes a lot of sense for reasons mentioned elsewhere in this book, but a lot of players prefer D20 or D18. Don't rule out any double and practice enough to where you are comfortable hitting all of them the same. If you find you have time left at the end of the session then concentrate on hitting the core doubles, which I designate as 20, 18, 16, 12, 10 and 8. These are the doubles you will find yourself on most of the time and are the ones that deserve special attention.

Let's break these down further and explain why we go for certain combinations over others and explain what gives you the best possible percentage chance of successful finishing:

Detail

2

Only one way to get this of course. A good rule is to throw the first dart high so it gives a good target for the second to go into the double.

3

Again, there is only one way to get this finish

4

D2 - S2, D1 if needed.

5
1, D2 or 3, D1.

Most players will use the first option because you have the further option of D1 if needed. If you go for 3, D1 there is no room for error.

6
D3 or 2, D2.

There are advantages and disadvantages to both these combinations. If you have all 3-darts available and go straight for it and hit the single, then you have the option of 1, D1 (as you have 3 remaining). However, if you miss on the outside of the wire with your first dart and then single the second, all you can do is hit the single 1 to set up a double on the next turn – which you may never get a shot at if your opponent takes out the finish.

Going for 2, D2 means that you guarantee 2 darts at a double (assuming you don't miss the single 2), but at the expense of losing one of the darts in your hand. With the first option of going straight for it you have the potential of 3 darts at the double. With the second option of 2, D2 you only have 2 darts at the double, which decreases your percentage of hitting a winning double.

With 2 darts in your hand it is better to go straight for it. If you break it down to 2, D2 you are only leaving yourself one dart to hit the double, which means there is no room for error. At least by going straight for it you give yourself two possible chances to finish.

With one dart left you have no choice but to go straight for it unless your opponent is so far back they aren't even on a finish.

Which way to go with all three darts in your hand is always a hot topic for debate and depends how you feel on any given day. As with all the finishing combinations, practice all of them to find the ones that you are most comfortable with. Knowing there are alternatives will add to your armory and will help your confidence grow as you improve through consistent practice.

7
3, D2.

It is always possible to throw for 5, D1 but this is not recommended because you always want to leave a double that will breakdown to other doubles if possible. As always, there are exceptions as you will see as the finishes develop in the following chapters.

8

D4. Breaks down to D2 and D1 if required.

9
1, D4.

Be careful with this because if you miss the S1 on either side you will bust your score. There is also the option of 5, D2 and 7, D1 but neither of these is recommended for two reasons:

Firstly, the golden rule is that wherever possible leave doubles that break down easily. By leaving D2 you are ignoring a very good double in D4 and lowering your percentage odds of taking out the finish. You lower the odds even more by going for the 7, D1 option.

The second reason why you should not go for either of the alternative options is that the numbers either side of the required singles (5 or 7) will also result in a bust score. I mention these alternatives just to show you that there are always plenty of options. Choosing the right one is key to mastering the finishes.

10
D5 or 2, D4.

Refer to the finish of 6 above. The same principles apply here.

11

3, D4.

As in 9 above, be careful when throwing for the single number. Many players are so intent on hitting the double that they forget to concentrate on hitting the single first and end up busting their score. Always have full concentration on every aspect of the finish and not just the final double.

12

D6 or 4, D4.

Like 6, although it is worth noting that D6 breaks down to D3 as well, so there is no advantage to be gained by going for the 4, D4 option. I included it once again to show there are always options. Choosing the right one is key. I make no apologies for repeatedly stating this, because choosing the correct option is absolutely the number one skill that will either make or break you when it comes to finishing consistently and confidently.

13

5, D4

1, D6 works as well, but 5, D4 is the better option because of the way the doubles break down. You may see patterns emerging even at this early stage, and if you do then you are correct. There are patterns in finishing and once you recognize them everything begins to become clearer and making the right choices becomes easier.

14

D7 or 6, D4.

Refer to 6 above as the same principles apply here.

15
7, D4 or 3, D6

7, D4 is the preferred method because of the way the doubles break down. Lots of players use the 3, D6 route, and this is fine if is your preferred method.

16

D8. Every time

17
1, D8 or 9, D4.

There are always exceptions to the rules and this is one of them. The patterns of this method clearly show that 1, D8 is the way to go, and you would be absolutely right to go for it this way. However, the alternative of 9, D4 is an attractive way to go for the following reason:

If you went the conventional way and missed either side of the S1 then you would bust your score, and the throw (and possibly game and match) is over.

By going for 9, D4, you have some leeway with the surrounding single numbers. A dart that dropped into the single 14 would give the chance to finish on 1, D1. If you miss above into the single 12, it would give you a chance to finish 5 (1, D2 or 3, D1). So, depending on how confident you are at throwing for a single will answer which path to choose.

18
D9 or 2, D8. See 6 above.

19
3, D8 or 11, D4.

The same applies here as in 17 above. Going 3, D8 is the recognized way to go for 19, and you will see many players always using this combination. However, if you miss to the left and hit 19, you have burst your score. A miss to the right and you have hit 17, leaving you with D1.

If you use 11, D4, then you have more leeway if you stray into the singles either side of 11. If you drop into 8 then you require 11 (3, D4), and if you go above into 14 you will leave 5 (1, D2).

20

D10. Always

21

5, D8 - 1, D10 - 13, D4

The obvious and most popular method here is 5, D8 for all the reasons mentioned above. D8 breaks down nicely all the way to D1 without having to split it.

13, D4 does have one advantage, and that's because the 13 and 4 segments are right next door to each other. If you hit S13 you don't have to readjust to the other side of the dartboard to hit the double; it's right next door. Left-handed players often prefer the right-hand side of the board, so the 13, D4 route may work better for you.

Another good route for left handed players, or any player that prefers the D20, D10 route is to go for 1, D10.

Every one of these methods allows room for error on the double so all of them are viable ways to go. Pick your favorite and be aware of the others as another piece of your finishing armory.

22

D11 – 6, D8 - 2, D10

See 6 above for explanations regarding going straight for an odd double versus splitting it down to a good double. Going for D8 or D10 is a personal choice.

23
7, D8 - 3, D10

Generally, 7, D8 is the recommended method, but left-handed players or those who prefer the D20, D10 may prefer going this way.

24

D12 Always

25
9, D8 - 5, D10 - 1, D12 - 17, D4

9, D8 is the highest recommendation, but for reasons mentioned above 5, D10 or 17, D4 may be preferable. If D12 is a favored double then 1, D12 is also a popular choice. As always, practice them all and find your preference. By knowing other alternatives, you will always hold an advantage and you will be able to finish from anywhere on the board.

26
D13 - 10, D8 - 6, D10 - 2, D12

See 6 above if you are not sure about whether to go straight for it or to break it down.

If you prefer to break it down, then going for the big wedge of 6/10 is a very good choice. They are right next door to each other, and present a big target, so setting up the double should present no problems.

27
11, D8 - 7, D10 - 3, D12 - 19, D4

Although the 11, D8 route is widely popular, this is a situation where 3, D12 may be beneficial. Whenever possible always go for the percentage shot, and this shot gives more room for error than any of the others.

Because the S3 and S19 are next to each other, you have a large area to aim at. If you hit the S3, then D12 is a good double to leave yourself on. If you stray over to the 19, then D4 is left, and that is also a good double to leave yourself on. Even if you stray to the right and hit the S17 you are still able to finish on D5 (although this is not recommended if you can help it).

28
D14 - 12, D8 - 8, D10 - 4, D12

D14 breaks down to D7 so you are wasting a dart if you try to break it down to a more preferred double. Going straight for D14 is the recommended route. As before, I present options, so you are aware that they exist, but for this shot always go straight for D14.

29
13, D8 - 9, D10 - 5, D12

13, D8 is always going to be the most popular route, but there are other options.

Going for 5, D12 may give you an advantage as they are next door to each other, meaning there is less adjustment when throwing at the double.

For left-handed throwers, or players that prefer the right-hand side of the board, 9, D10 is another good option.

30
D15 - 14, D8 - 6, D12 - 10, D10

See 6 above. Going for 10, D10 gives an advantage in that it is the same segment. If going this route, make sure that you don't block the double with your first dart. There is also the danger of bursting your score by hitting the T10 so be careful.

Going straight for it is always a good option, so never discard this just because you are facing an odd double.

31
15, D8 - 7, D12 - 11, D10

The first option is recommended for most players. For left-handed players, or people that prefer the right-hand side of the board, 11, D10 is a good option

32

D16 Always

33
1, D16 - 17, D8 - 9, D12 - 13, D10

D16 and D20 are probably the most important doubles on the dartboard, and you have now reached the point where one of them comes into play (D16). As always though, it isn't the only option! 1, D16 is probably the way most players would go for this shot, and there is nothing wrong with that. A slip either way still leaves a finish (13 if you hit 20 and 15 if you hit 18). A good alternative is to go for 17, D8. A slip to the left and you are still on a double (15). A slip to the right still leaves 31, and therefore a possible finish. For this reason, going for 17, D8 is the most recommended way of getting this: It gives you more room for error on the single number, and the double breaks down well.

For left-handed players or people who prefer the right side of the board, 13, D10 is a good option.

9, D12 is another good example where the numbers are next to each other, so less adjustment is required. This makes it a good option to consider too.

34
D17 - 2, D16 - 10, D12 - 14, D10

The dilemma between going straight for a double as opposed to breaking it down is explained in finish 6 above. If you do prefer to break it down then 2, D16 is the preferred option unless you are left handed or would rather throw at the right side of the board.

35
3, D16 - 19, D8 - 11, D12 - 15, D10

The 3/19 route is definitely the way to go here. If you miss to the left then you hit S19, which leaves D8. If you hit the 3 you are left with D16. Even if you miss to the right you are still on a finish, although D9 is often considered the worst double on the dartboard. However, if you practice all the doubles as explained at the beginning of this chapter then D9 will hold no fear for you. You will be able to hit every double, no matter where it is on the dartboard.

For left-handed players, or those who prefer the right side of the board, 15, D10 is a good option because they are next to each other, which means there is less readjustment required when moving from the single to the double.

36

D18 Always.

37
5, D16 - 1, D18 - 13, D12 - 17, D10

5, D16 is the recommended way to go for this finish.

For people who like D18 (many players have D18 as their favorite double, but are careful as it only breaks down one time to D9. Other options allow more room for error), the numbers are next to each other so there is less room for adjustment.

For left-handed players, or people who prefer the right-hand side of the board, 17, D10 is a good option.

13, D12 is a good option for those who like the D12.

38
D19 - 6, D16 - 2, D18 - 14, D12 - 18, D10

If you prefer to break it down, then 6, D16 is the recommended way to go. I make no apologies for continually repeating that D16 and D20 are the best doubles on the dartboard, and it is highly recommended to leave them whenever possible. When given the choice between D20 or D16, it depends on the personal preferences of the individual throwing at the finish.

One exception is when you are sat on an odd double with 3 darts in your hand. Then you have the option of either going straight for it or throwing a dart at a single number to leave your preferred double. Pick your poison!

The other options are for those who prefer D18, D12 or D10.

39
7, D16 - 3, D18 - 15, D12 - 19, D10

7, D16 is definitely preferred here. Not only is it one of the two best doubles on the dartboard, but the numbers 7 and 16 are right next to each other. This is highly recommended as the way to go for this combination. If your dart strays to the right and lands in the S19, then D10 is left too.

40
D20 Always.

Chapter 1 Quiz

Now that you have practiced every finish from 2-40 and have learned all the combinations presented in this chapter, it is time to test yourself before you move on.

Make sure you can answer all these questions without having to involve mental mathematics. They should be learned one by one. Done this way, you will know every finish below the current number you are working on easily and effortlessly.

Here is an example. You require 37, and you automatically know that the combination is 5, D16. You throw at S5 and drop down into S12. Now you require 25. Instinctively you throw at 9, D8. No drama, no hesitation.

Eventually you will not even have to work out what is left if you miss the big single number because you will have done it so many times that it becomes ingrained into your brain. By learning just one finish at a time it breaks it down into manageable chunks that is easily learned and absorbed.

1. Describe 2 ways to go for 17. Which is your preferred way to go and why?
2. Describe 3 ways to go for 21. What are the benefits of each route? Which do you prefer? Why?
3. You require 22. Explain the pros and cons of going straight for the finish against breaking it down to a better double.
4. You require 26 with 2 darts in your hand. Do you go straight for it or break it down to a more suitable double? Why?
5. Describe 4 ways to get 25. Explain the benefits of each method.
6. You require 27. You decide to go for 3, D12 as it leaves D4 if you miss to the left and hit a S19. However, you hit T3. What is left and how would you go for it? Why?

7. Demonstrate 4 ways of going for 27. Which way do you prefer? Why? What are the benefits of each route?
8. You require 34 with 3 darts in your hand. Which way would you go and why?
9. Explain the benefit of going for 3, D16 when requiring 35. Why is there a good margin for error with this method?
10. You require 26 with 2 darts left in your hand. Which way are you going and why?
11. Congratulations! You now have the knowledge and experience to move on to the next chapter. Don't stop practicing these lower finishes because they are a vital part of your ammunition. Knowing them and being able to hit them are two very different things, and for the latter to happen on a consistent basis you need the 3 P's – practice, practice and practice!

I hope that by now you will have learned that even the simplest of finishing combinations are not as simple as you first envisioned.

It's one thing to just have a list of finishes and learn to throw a certain way for each one. This method teaches another, complete step-by-step method, with different ways to go for each finish.

By not only learning the finishes, *but to also understanding the why behind the how,* you will gain a much deeper understanding of how it all works and will be a much better player because of it.

Chapter Two: 41-60

Here are the finishes you will be working on in this chapter:

Number	Solution
41	9, D16 1, D20 5, D18 17, D12
42	10, D16 2, D20 6, D18 18, D12
43	11, D16 3, D20 7, D18 19, D12
44	12, D16 4, D20 8, D18 20, D12
45	13, D16 5, D20 9, D18
46	14, D16

	6, D20 10, D18
47	15, D16 7, D20 11, D18
48	16, D16 8, D20 12, D18
49	17, D16 9, D20 13, D18
50	18, D16 10, D20 14, D18 B
51	19, D16 11, D20 15, D18
52	20, D16 12, D20 16, D18
53	13, D20 17, D18
54	14, D20 18, D18
55	15, D20 19, D18

56	16, D20
	20, D18
57	17, D20
	O/B, D16
58	18, D20
59	19, D20
60	20, D20

Practice Sessions

Always warm up first to get your arm going, and then do the doubles practice routine as outlined in chapter 1 before moving onto the main focus of the day's practice.

In this chapter you are going to concentrating on the finishes 41 to 60. Although you have moved above the one dart finishes, the out shots detailed here - along with those in chapter 1 - are the most important ones you will ever learn. Even if you only studied and mastered these first two chapters and nothing else, you would become a fearsome finisher and a very dangerous opponent.

Detail

41

9, D16 - 1, D20 - 5, D18 - 17, D12

9, D16 is the most popular way to go for this finish, and it is the recommended method. For those that prefer D20, the advantage is that the numbers are side by side so there are fewer adjustments to be made. The other options are for those who prefer D18 or D12.

42
10, D16 - 2, D20 - 6, D18 - 18, D12

This is one of those occasions where the board is kind to you. You have a huge target at 10/6 to aim at, virtually guaranteeing you 2 darts at a double. So, this is definitely the recommended method of going for this finish. Whenever the board presents itself to you like this, it is always the best option to take advantage of it. For those who prefer D20, then 2, D20 is the way to go.

43
3, D20 - 19, D12 - 11, D16 - 7, D18

As with the finish above, this is another great opportunity to guarantee two darts at a double. In fact, with this finish, you have 3 singles side by side that all leave a good double to finish on. 3, D20, 19, D12 or 7, D18 are all good finishes. Even if you go for the 3, D20 and miss to the right and hit S17 you still have a finish, although it is far from ideal as it leaves D13. So, 3, D20 or 19, D12 is the recommended way to go here. For once, going for D16 is the least favored method because it leaves no room for error.

44
12, D16 - 4, D20 - 8, D18 - 20, D12

12, D16 is the most common method here, although 4, D20 is very popular as well. This one is down to personal preference.

45
13, D16 - 5, D20 - 9, D18

13, D16 is the most popular method with this finish, although 5, D20 does have an advantage for those who prefer D20. The 5 and 20 are next to each other so there is less adjustments to be made when throwing for the double. The vast majority of players will throw for the 13, D16.

46
14, D16 - 6, D20 - 10, D18

This is another of those times when the board offers you an advantage, and when it does you should take it. The 10/6 is a huge target and virtually guarantees you two darts at a double. When you reach the stage in your game when you are confident of your throw and you rarely miss the big singles then 14, D16 may be the way for you to go, but until then take advantage of the board and play the percentages. Go for the 6/10 wedge and guarantee yourself two darts at the double.

47
15, D16 - 7, D20 - 11, D18

15, D16 is by far the most popular method of getting this finish. 7, D20 is there for those who prefer the D20 route, and 11, D18 for those who prefer the D18.

48
16, D16 - 8, D20 - 12, D18

48 is a great finish to leave yourself on because the 16/8 wedge guarantees you 2 darts at a double, and these are the best two doubles on the entire dartboard! Unless you just love D18 there is absolutely no reason to throw anywhere other than at the 16/8 wedge on this finish. One word of caution: If you go for 16, D16, make sure you don't hit the T16 by mistake. This happens more times than it should, so be careful.

49
17, D16 - 9, D20 - 13, D18

17, D16 is the most popular method of getting this finish. 9, D20 is there for those who prefer that route and the same goes for the 13, D18. As in all these finishes, be careful of hitting the treble when going for the big single numbers. If you accidentally stray into the T17 when throwing for 49 you have burst your score.

If you are going for 9, D20 and hit the T9 you will be on 22, and if you hit T13 when going for 13, D18 you will be left with 10.

50
18, D16 - 10, D20 - 14, D18 - B

This is the first time the bullseye has come into play, and you often see players throwing for it when they have three or two darts in their hands. Let me make it clear right here and now that unless you are trying to impress someone (or yourself), NEVER throw at the bullseye with 2 or 3 darts in your hand.

Only throw at the bullseye with 1 dart in your hand, and even then, only if your opponent is on a finish. Otherwise set it up for a good double next time around. Finishing is a percentage game, and you want the odds as much in your favor as possible. It is difficult enough so don't showboat and make it even harder for yourself. Many players have lost games by going for the bullseye when there was no need to. The usual story is that they miss it and leave an obscure finish, and then end up at double one. By this time their opponent is down to a finish and nails it first dart. You have been warned.

18, D16 is the most common way to go for this finish, but beware of hitting the T18 as you will burst your score. 10, D20 may be a better method for just that reason. If you hit the T10 you are on D10, which is a good combination. 14, D18 is for those who prefer D18.

51
19, D16 - 11, D20 - 15, D18

19, D16 is the most popular method of getting this finish. Just be careful not to hit the T19 as it would burst your score. If you go right into S3 then you require 48. If you hit T3 then you require 42. Go left into S7 and you are left with 44. Hit T7 and you require 30.

How To Master The Art Of Finishing

11, D20 is the way to go if you prefer the D20/D10 route. If you hit T11 then you require 18, which is not desirable. If you drop down into S8 then you will require 43. Hit T8 and you require 27. Go high into S14 and you will require 37. T14 leaves 9.

If you prefer to go the D18 route then 15, D8 is the way to go. If you slip into T15 then you will require 6. Go high into single 10 and you will require 41. Hit T10 and you will require 21. Drop into S2 and you will require 49. T2 leaves you on 45.

I added the "where to go if you miss" finishes here to demonstrate the complexities of the art of finishing. I am not going to do it for every finish because you need to practice enough so that you rarely miss the big singles to set up the double.

Once we get to the point where we require a treble to set up a double then I will go into more detail of where to go if you miss the treble. The example here is to show you the importance of concentrating as hard on the big single as you do on the double at the end of the combination.

If you practice these finishes as recommended then you will quickly learn what to go for if you miss the big single, and you will instinctively know what to throw for each and every time. Be patient and stick with it. You will be surprised at how quickly you will learn all these finishes. If you have studies the book correctly so far, then you will already know how to take out a finish if the wrong single is hit because we have already covered the lower numbers!!!

52
20, D16 - 12, D20 – 16, D18

20, D16 is the most popular method of getting this finish, but beware of hitting the T20 as it will burst your score.

12, D20 is another very popular way of going for it. One benefit of going this way is that if you hit the T12 instead of the big single you will still be left on a good double because T12 leaves D8.

16, D18 is the way to go if you prefer D18. Hitting the T16 leaves you on D2 so be careful if you do decide to go this way.

53
13, D20 - 17, D18

D16 is no longer an option unless you waste an extra dart to set it up, and that is not a recommended course of action. So now the preferred shot is 13, D20. Be careful that you don't hit the T13 or you will be left with D7.

If you prefer to go the D18 route, then 17, D18 is your shot.

54
14, D20 - 18, D18

14, D20 is the most popular choice here. If you hit the T14 you will require 12 which isn't a bad leave.

18, D18 has the advantage of staying on the same number, but beware of hitting the T18 as it would burst your score.

55
15, D20 - 19, D18

15, D20 is the most popular way to get this finish.

19, D18 is a good option for those preferring D18, but be very careful of hitting the T19 as it would burst your score.

56
16, D20 - 20, D18

16, D20 is the most popular way of getting this finish. If you hit T16 you require 8, and if you go high into the T8 you will require 32, so this way is by far the most recommended way to go.

For those who prefer D18, even after all the advantages mentioned above, 20, D18 is your shot but be careful not to drop into the T20 or you will burst your score.

57
17, D20

17, D20 is the only viable way to go for this finish. Be careful not to hit the T17 as it will leave you on 6.

If you are trying to impress your friends, then you can go for the O/B, D16, but this is not a recommended way to go for this finish. Remember, you always want to go for the shots that give you the best possible chance of securing the finish. You want the odds on your side.

58
18, D20

18, D20 is the way to go for this finish. If you hit T18 you will be left on 4.

59
19, D20

19, D20 is the way to go for this finish. Be wary of hitting the T19 as it will leave you on D1.

60
20, D20

20, D20 is the way to go for this finish. You need to make sure you aim high at the single 20; otherwise your dart may slip into the T20 and burst your score.

If possible, try to throw the first dart high and to the side of the single 20 bed. That way, when you throw your next dart at the D20 your first dart won't be in the way.

Chapter 2 Quiz

1. Describe two ways you would go for 41. Which is your favorite and
2. why?
3. You step up to the board requiring 42. Your first dart goes high of the target and goes into T6. What are you left with?
4. Describe three ways you would take out 47. Which is your favorite and why?
5. Describe three ways you would take out 49. Which is your favorite and why?
6. You step up to the board with all three darts in your hand requiring 50. What should you NOT do in this situation, and why? More importantly, which way should you go for it?
7. You step up to the board requiring 53. You throw at 13, and your dart goes low, landing in single 6. What do you have left and how do you go for it?
8. Describe three ways you would take out 54. Which is your favorite and why?
9. You require 55 and your first dart goes into the T15. What is left and how do you go for it?
10. You require You require 54 and your first dart goes low into the single 4. You have 50 left with two darts. How would you go for it and why?
11. You have 60 left. What must you try to do with your first dart to make the next shot easier?

We have now reached the end of the two dart finishes, or at least the ones where no treble (or bull) is required first. These finishes are the foundations for everything that follows, and by *really* drilling these down, you are already two thirds of the way to knowing everything else that follows.

Chapter Three: 61-80

If you dedicate yourself to mastering the finishes from 2 to 80, and can hit them with a good degree of accuracy, not only will your confidence grow exponentially as a dart player, but you will be a feared competitor at almost any level. Other players will be wary of you, and will not want to leave you on any kind of finish because they know that the chances are you will take it out. That is when all the hours of practice, and all the hours of dedication and hard work you have put into this will begin to pay off.

The finishes detailed in this, and the previous chapters are the most important ones you will ever learn. The vast majority of your finishes will be in the 2-80 range, and when you can hit them with regularity and confidence, you will be in a position to take your game to whatever level your commitment and talent allows.

Another benefit of knowing all the finishes up to this point is that everything else that follows is easy to learn. All that follows is a combination of a big treble (or Bull) followed by one of the finishes in the 2-80 range. And you will already know those without even thinking about them. That is the beauty of this system and how each level of finishing builds upon the ones that have gone before.

Please note that I said the bigger finishes are easy to learn. Not easy to get! Even the very best players in the world get excited when they hit a big finish. There is no better feeling in darts (with the exception of winning the tournament you are playing in) than taking out a huge finish when your opponent is sat on a double. And nothing gets into the head of your opponent more than a player that takes out huge finishes at crucial times in a game. YOU will be that player after you have studied and practiced the methods in this book.

Here are the detailed finishes from 61-80:

It is imperative when going for finishes in this range that you leave yourself requiring 60 or less after the first dart. This ensures that you will get at least one dart at a double and won't have to either set it up for next time or throw at the bull to take it out. So, every finish in this chapter ensures that after the first dart is thrown, you are left on 60 or less.

Number	Solution
61	O/B, D18
	T15, D8
	T7, D20
	11, B
	T11, D14
62	T10, D16
	T14, D10
	T18, D4
	12, B
	T12, D13
63	T13, D12
	T17, D6
	T9, D18
	13, B
64	T16, D8
	T8, D20
	14, B
	T14, D11
65	O/B, D20
	T15, D10

		T11, D16
		T19, D4
		15, B
	66	T10, D18
		B, D8
		T14, D12
		16, B
		T16, D9
	67	T17, D8
		T9, D20
		17, B
	68	T20, D4
		T12, D16
		T16, D10
		18, B
		T18, D7
	69	T15, D12
		T19, D6
		T11, D18
		19, B
	70	T18, D8
		T10, D20
		20, B
		T20, D5
	71	T13, D16
		T17, D10
	72	T16, D12
		T12, D18

	T20, D6
73	T19, D8
	T11, D20
74	T14, D16
	T18, D10
75	T17, D12
	T13, D18
	O/B, B
76	T20, D8
	T12, D20
77	T19, D10
	T15, D16
78	T18, D12
	T14, D18
79	T19, D11
	T13, D20
80	T20, D10
	T16, D16

Details

As always, do the warm-up and practice sessions detailed in chapter one before moving onto the finishes.

61
O/B, D18 - T15, D8

There are two popular ways to go for this finish, and with three darts either is fine. Going the OB, D18 gets the nod because the outer bull is a big target, and then you will have two clear darts at double 18. The big danger here is, ironically, being too accurate. It's one of those occasions where you want to avoid the bullseye and just hit the outer ring. If you hit the bullseye, then you are left with 11. You see this happen to the world's best players on television quite often, and it will happen to you as well if you throw at it often enough. It's okay though – because you have practiced the previous chapters diligently, you know without missing a beat that you need 3, D4 to complete the finish. Finishing is all about percentages, and you need to give yourself as many darts at a double as possible, so hopefully you won't hit the bullseye when going for the outer bull!

The other recommended route is T15, D8. You see players like Phil Taylor go for it this way when they have three darts in their hands.

If you miss the T15 and hit the single (which you are much more likely to do), then you will be left with 46 with two darts left in your hand. You could go 14, D16, and this is perfectly acceptable, but bearing in mind that you want to play the percentages as much as possible, it is better to go for the big 6/10 wedge and assure yourself of at least one dart at a double. Hitting 6 leaves you D20, and hitting 10 leaves you D18, both good doubles.

T7, D20 is a way of going for it that you are seeing more and more with players like James Wade. If D20 is your favorite double then there is nothing wrong with going for it this way.

If you single 7 then you will need 54. Bearing in mind that you went for T7 with the sole intention of leaving D20, and then it makes sense that you will stay with this and go for 14, D20 with two darts left.

If you miss to the right and hit 19 then you will need 42. If you miss to the left and hit big 16, then you will be left on 45.

11, B. This is ONLY to be thrown for if you have two darts left in your hand AND your opponent is on a finish. It is used a lot in higher three dart combinations as you will see later. This also introduces the possibility of going T11, D14. Again, this is only to be done if you have two darts in your hands.

Going for the treble/double combination is a little trickier because the single segment is narrower where the treble bed is as opposed to near the double bed. This means that it is much easier to drop into the singles either side of 11 if you go for the treble. If you are in even the slightest doubt, ignore the treble altogether and go for the biggest part of the single bed. That way you are guaranteed a dart at the bull. Even if you then miss the bull and lose the leg, at least you had a dart to win it rather than just setting it up for the next time around.

62

T10, D16 - T14, D10 - T18, D4 - 12, B - T12, D13

There are three main ways to go for this, and all of them have their merits. Let's start with the most popular, T10, D16. It's easy to see why people prefer this way as it keeps the percentages on our side and lands us on the most popular double on the board. For this reason, this is the recommended way to get this. If you hit single 10 you are left with 52.

Left-handed players tend to prefer the right-hand side of the board, and if this is you then T14, D10 will be your choice. James Wade goes for 62 this way, and he is deadly on D10. If you hit the single 14 then you are left with 48, which is a good shot with two darts because you can throw at the big wedge of 16/8 to leave either D16 or D20.

How To Master The Art Of Finishing

A less popular option is T18, D4. Jelle Klaasen goes for it this way, as does Gary Anderson on occasion. It does have its merits. If you go into the single 18 you are left with 44, which is a good 2- dart out. 4 is right next door to 18 and it is an easy adjustment to hit single 4 for D20.

Everything written above regarding the 61 finish with two darts in your hand applies to all the finishes from 61-70 in this section. ONLY throw 12, B when you have two darts in your hands and your opponent is on a finish. Anything else is showboating and can cost you the leg, and possibly the match. The same applies to T12, D13 as this is part of the same combination.

63

T13, D12 – T17, D6 – T9, D18 – 13, B

Most players will go for T13, D12 with this finish. It's the same shot with two darts in your hand as well. Just remember that if you have three darts and you hit single 13 with the first one, you DO NOT throw for the bull. Instead, go for 18, D16, or 10, D20, or even 14, D18. Only throw for the bull if you have one dart left in your hand and your opponent is on a finish.

Here's a scenario: Let's say that you are on 63 and your opponent is on 168. You throw for T13 and get a bounce out. So now you still have 63 and have two darts left. What do you do?

The first thing you always do is check to see where your opponent is in relation to the game. If he is on a finish the answer is simple -you go right back at the T13 again. If you hit the single, then you throw for the bullseye to try to win the leg.

In this scenario your opponent is on 168, which you will discover later is one of the "bogey numbers" that is not a finish. In this case you have a choice. You would still go back for the T13 with the second dart, and if you hit it then all is good, and you throw for the D12. If you hit the single 13 then you have a choice, and it is purely a personal one. Do you want the glory? Go for the bullseye. Do you want to pragmatic and play the averages? Set it up for the double when you return to the oche.

T17, D6 is a way I have seen players throw for it, and there is nothing wrong with going this way if this is what you prefer.

There are two schools of thought with this scenario. The first one is that leaving D12 is a better option because it breaks down nicely to D6 before going to the less than optimum D3. In that regard, going T13, D12 is a better option than going for T17, D6.

The other school of thought is that you throw for T17 way more than T13, so therefore you should probably have a better chance of hitting it. If this is true, then this may be the better way of going for it. Either way, you will see most players going the T13, D12 route. This is the one that is most recommended.

If you do opt for the T17, D6 route and you hit the single 17, then you are left with 46. You could go 14, D16, but a good option here would be to throw for the big wedge of 6/10 to leave D20 or D18.

64
T16, D8 – T8, D20 – 14, B – T14, D11

This is a good finish to leave as it gives you a great chance of setting it up no matter where your first dart lands, as long as it is in the 16/8 wedge. You will see this finish being left many times by the top players in tournaments.

T16, D8 is the favored way to go, but it is good to aim for the wire separating the T8 and T16. This gives you a big target to aim at and gives you a great chance of hitting the treble with the first dart. If you hit single 16, then you are on 48, which is single 16 again and D16. Just be careful that you don't hit the T16 with the second dart and burst your score.

Hit single 8 with the first dart and you are on 56. Now you have to hit the single 16 to leave D20. If you hit the T16 with the second dart, you will require D4, so any of these leaves a good finish. Of course, you could always go for 20, D18 if you your first dart hits the single 8, but you are already aiming at the 16/8 wedge so why move?

Going for the 14, B or T14, D11 is only to be done when you have two darts left and your opponent is sitting on a finish.

I hope you can see the patterns emerging all over the dartboard by now. With regular practice and studying these finishes, all the mathematics will be removed from the situation and you will know instinctively what to throw for every time, just like the Pro's. It really is not difficult once you start to recognize the patterns and learn the combinations.

For example, you may have noticed the nice symmetry between the finishes of 61 and 64 when you have two darts left in your hands. This comes much more into play when you are throwing for the finishes in the 120+ area, and we will get to those shortly. For now, though, just notice that when throwing for 61 and you hit T11, it leaves D14, and when you throw for 64 and you hit T14 it leaves D11. By recognizing these patterns, it allows you to remember them more easily the next time you encounter them.

65

O/B, D20 – T15, D10 – T11, D16 - T19, D4 - 15, B

With three darts available, almost everyone chooses to go the O/B, D20 route with this shot. Why? Because the bullseye is a big target, and hitting the outer ring gives you two clear darts at one of the major doubles on the board – D20. Over all the other ways to get this finish, going this way just makes the most sense.

This is what I mean by not being a slave to any one particular double – especially double 16. Sure, you can throw for T11, D16, and this is a viable way to go for it because hitting single 11 leaves you on 54.

But the percentages are better if you go the O/B, D20 route, and this is the recommended way to go for this.

T19, D4 is a viable way to go for it, because hitting single 19 will leave you on 46, which is best served by going for the big 10/6 wedge to ensure you get a dart at a double. However, I have rarely, if ever, seen anyone throw for 65 in this manner because the O/B, D20 is the better percentage shot.

T15, D10 is another viable way of going for this, but it is worth noting that even fabled D10 proponent James Wade will go for the O/B on this shot.

Try not to hit the bullseye when throwing for the O/B (which you inevitably will; it happens to all of us). If you do then you will require 15, which is still viable with 2 darts left in your hand.

15, B is the way to go if you have two darts in your hands and your opponent is on a finish.

66
T10, D18 – B, D8 – T14, D12 – 16, B – T16, D9

Any of the first three ways work for this finish. T10, D18 is probably the most used way to go for it. Single 10 leaves you with 56, which is either 16, D20 or 20, D18.

T14, D12 is less frequently used than the T10 route, but it is still a good way to go for it. Single 14 will leave 52, which is a good 2 dart finish.

B, D8 is used more and more these days, and the reason is because the bull is a big target. Bullseye leaves D8, and the O/B leaves 41, which is a good 2 dart out-shot. Players such as Phil Taylor use this method regularly.

Going for the 16, B or T16, D9 is only to be done when you have two darts in your hands and your opponent is on a finish.

67
T17, D8 – T9, D20 – 17, B

T17, D8 is by far the most popular way to go for this finish, and is the recommended way to go for it. Single 17 leaves 50; which you will get by going either 18, D16, 10, D20, or 14, D18. I know you weren't planning on going for the bullseye with two darts left in your hands!!

T9, D20 is for the diehard D20 fans, although it goes back to being a slave to a particular double. Single 9 will leave 58, which is 18, D20. There is nothing wrong with this shot but the T17 route is the way the vast majority of players would go for this shot.

17, B is only for – you guessed it – when you have two darts in your hands and your opponent is on a finish.

68
T20, D4 – T12, D16 - T16, D10 – 18, B – T18, D7

T20 is the number you throw at more than anything else on the entire dartboard, so it makes sense for you to throw at it again here. As always, it comes down to the percentages; you probably have a better percentage chance of hitting the T20 than any other treble on the board. For that reason, T20, D4 is the recommended way to go for this shot. Single 20 will leave 48, which enables you to throw at the big 16/8 wedge.

T12, D16 is another good way to go for this shot. Single 12 will leave 56, which is a popular 2-dart finish to leave.

T16, D10 is a favorite of James Wade, and left-handed players may prefer to go this way. Single 16 leaves a finish of 52.

18, B or T18, D7 is only for the two-dart scenario outlined repeatedly in this book.

69
T15, D12 – T19, D6 – T11, D18 – 19, B

T15, D12 is probably the most popular way to go for this, but T19, D6 is very close behind. The reason is that T19 is thrown at more than T15. Either way is fine. Practice them both and pick your favorite.

If you go T15, then the single leaves 54, which is 14, D20 or 18, D18. If you go for T19 then single leaves 50. I know you are going to go for either 10, D20, 18, D16 or 14, D18.

19, B or T19, D6 is for the two-dart scenario.

70
T18, D8 – T10, D20 – 20, B – T20, D5

T18, D8 or T10, D20 are equally recommended here. It is down to personal preference which way you go. Both are great ways to get this finish. Single 18 will leave 52, and single 10 leaves 60.

20, B or T20, D5 is to be used in the two-dart scenario.

All the numbers from 61-70 can be finished in two darts by hitting a single number and then the bullseye (for instance 68 – 18, B). From 71-80, unless you hit a treble with the first dart, they are all three dart finishes.

71
T13, D16 – T17, D10

T13, D16 is the way most go for this finish. If you hit single 13 then you need 58.

T17, D10 is the favored way of left-handed players such as James Wade. Single 17 will leave 54.

72
T16, D12 – T12, D18 – T20, D6

The first two are the favored finishes for this combination although more and more you are seeing players going for the T20, D6 combination. This is because they throw at 20 all the time and have more confidence of hitting it than other trebles on the board.

If you go the T16, D12 route and hit single 16, you then need 56, which will leave single 16 again for D20. For this reason, this is the preferred way to go for this finish.

If you go the T12, D18 route, then a single 12 leaves 60, which is 20, D20.

If you do decide to go the T20, D6 route, then single 20 leaves 52, which is a very good 2 dart out-shot.

73
T19, D8 – T11, D20

T19, D8 is the only way to go for this. Single 19 will leave 54, which is a good 2 dart finish.

The reason T11, D20 is not recommended is because hitting single 11 does not leave you on 60 or below, which is our golden rule on finishes from 61-80. Hitting single 11 leaves 62, which with two darts left means having to throw for 12, B, or T12, D13. I put it here for completeness, and to show you that there are almost always other possibilities if you know the dartboard well enough.

74
T14, D16 – T18, D10

The majority of players would go for the T14, D16 with this shot. Left-handers tend to opt for the T18, D10 route.

If you hit the single 14, you will be on 60. If you go for the T18, D10 shot and hit the single 18, you will be on 56.

75
T17, D12 – T13, D18 – O/B, B

The only way here with three darts is T17, D12. If you hit single 17, you will require 58, which is 18, D20.

Going any other way would violate our rule of leaving 60 or below with two darts left if you hit the big single, so they are not recommended finishes when you have three darts in your hand. Single 13 will leave 62.

Going for the O/B, B route is a difficult shot that is best taken on when you have 2 darts in your hands, and your opponent is on a finish.

76
T20, D8 - T12, D20

T20, D8 is the only way to go here. Single 20 will leave 56, which is either 16, D20 or single 20 again for D18.

If you went the T12, D20 route and hit the single 12, you would require 64, which is above 60 so is not recommended. Again, it is here for clarity and completeness.

77
T19, D10 – T15, D16

T19, D10 is the only way to go here. Single 19 will leave 58, which is 18, D20.

Going for the T15 and hitting the big single leaves 62, so is not recommended.

78
T18, D12 – T14, D18

T18, D12 is the only way here. Single 18 leaves 60, which is 20, D20.

Hitting the big 14 when going for the treble leaves 64. Not recommended.

79
T19, D11 – T13, D20

This is the first time that conventional wisdom is turned on its head. Almost all standard out-shot charts will tell you to go for the T13, D20 in this situation. However, this is completely wrong and will only set you up to lose the leg, and possibly the match.

The reason is that if you hit the single 13 – and the law of averages states that you will do that more often than you will hit the treble – you will require 66, which violates our rule with this set of finishes. You would then have to hit 16, B or T16, D9 to win the leg, and that is just making it a whole lot harder for yourself.

As I stated in the introduction, there are always exceptions to the rules of going for the preferred finishes, and this is one of them. Sometimes going for the odd double is the correct choice of shot, and this is the first example of this in action.

If you hit single 19, you will require 60, which stays true to our rules and requires you to hit 20, D20. If you hit the T19 then just go straight for the D11. If you follow the practice guidelines in this book you will have practiced all the doubles on the board, and all of them will be accessible to you.

80
T20, D10 – T16, D16

T20, D10 is the way to go here. Single 20 will leave you on 60, which is S20 for D20. If your first dart does hit the single 20; be careful to throw high and away from the treble with your second dart, otherwise you may end up bursting your score.

Mervyn King is the only Pro I have seen going for T16, D16 when he has three darts in his hands. It means that if he hits the big 16, he then has to go for 14, B, or T14, D11. Neither is ideal, and this method is not recommended.

Chapter 3 Quiz

1. You have 61 remaining and you decide to go the O/B, D18 route. Your first dart misses the bull and goes into single 7. What do you have left, and how will you go for it?
2. You are sitting on 62. You throw for T10 to leave D16, but your dart goes high into the T6. What do you have left and how will you go for it?
3. You have 63 remaining. Your opponent is on 171. Your first dart hits the wire of T13 and bounces out. What do you do next?
4. You are sitting on 65. Which way are you going to go for this finish and why?
5. You are in a really close, tight game. Your opponent has just missed a dart at D16 to win the match. You walk up to the oche requiring 71. You prefer to go the T17, D10 route, and this what you throw for. Your first dart goes way off the mark and flies into the single 2. What do you have left, and what do you do next?
6. You require 72. Describe two ways of getting this finish and think about which of them would be your preferred option.
7. You are on 75 with three darts in your hand. How will you approach this finish? What would you do if you only had two darts left in your hand?
8. You are on 79. How will you go for this finish and why?
9. You are on 80. Your first dart lands just high of the treble in the single 20. What must you be careful of with the second dart and how will you approach it?
10. You are on 80 and your first dart landed off target to the left in the single 5. Your opponent is on 32. What do you have left and how are you going to go for it?

Congratulations! You have now learned the most important finishes you will ever encounter. Matches are won and lost with the finishes we have covered up to this point. The vast majority of the finishes you will ever hit will be in the 2-80 range, and it is vital that you get these finishes down so that you know them without even thinking. If you practice them diligently they will reward you many times over when it comes to game time.

If you industriously work your way through these first three chapters and get these finishes deep inside your head so they become as instinctive as putting on a pair of socks, and practice them repeatedly until you can hit them confidently and with regularity, you will become a feared and respected player. Your reputation will soar, and you will win a lot more than you lose. You will enter every match knowing that if it comes down to a close game you will have the edge because you can hit the finishes.

Even if you stopped at this point and never read another word in this book, you would know more than 99% of all dart players out there, and you would have the edge over many of your rivals. You would be a very accomplished player with a much higher than average knowledge of the art of finishing, and you would be the go to "expert" wherever you went to play.

You don't want to stop here though. You want to be the complete player and possess expert knowledge and skill with every finish, no matter what it is. That's why you bought this book. So give yourself a pat on the back for getting this far, roll up your sleeves, and let's get back to work!

Chapter Four: 81-90

From now onwards, if you want to leave a double you either have to hit a treble as a part of the combination, or be a bit more creative in your shot selection. It is also at this stage where the bullseye begins to come more into play. It is vital to be aware of where your opponent is in relation to the game, and your tactics and strategy have to be honed to a much higher level than before. You are now entering the world of the professional level of finishing knowledge.

Number	Solution
81	T19, D12 T15, D18
82	B, D16 T14, D20
83	T17, D16
84	T20, D12 T16, D18
85	T15, D20 T19, D14
86	T18, D16 B, D18
87	T17, D18

88	T20, D14
	T16, D20
89	T19, D16
90	T20, D15
	T18, D18
	B, D20

Details

As always, do the warm-up and practice sessions detailed in chapter one before moving onto the finishes.

81
T19, D12 – T15, D18

Most players go for this finish with the T19, D12 route. T19 is used in the scoring phase of the game as a cover shot, and is practiced much more than T15. It also leaves a very good double – D12. Even Dave Chisnall – a prolific D18 hitter – goes for 81 in this manner with three darts. So it is the recommended way to go for this finish.

If you hit the single 19 then you need 62. This is where the bullseye becomes much more important in your shot selection, as it is an integral part of the combination. With two darts left and your opponent on a finish, you will go for 12, B. If you hit the T12 then you will require D13. One thing to be aware of here (and with all the subsequent finishes in this chapter) is that if you decide to try to hit the T12, D13 shot, you are much more likely to drift into either of the 5 or 9 segments. This is because the scoring segment is much narrower in the area of the treble, and requires a much greater level of accuracy.

A lot of players, even the top professionals on television, ignore the treble option completely, and throw for the biggest part of the single.

This ensures that they will get one dart at the bull for the game. As always with finishing, you need to keep the percentages in your favor as much as you can. These finishes are difficult enough as it is, so you have to keep the odds on your side as much as possible.

The finishes in this chapter also bring up an interesting twist in how we can go for them. In this instance, we require 81. If you go for the bull with the first dart and hit either the bullseye or the O/B, you can set it up so that you have one dart at a double rather than throwing for the bull. This method is recommended only when your opponent is not on a finish, but it is a good option in those situations. Please note that this strategy only works on the finishes between 81 and 85.

The reason it is not recommended when it is a close game and your opponent is right there with you on a finish is that you will only be guaranteeing yourself one dart at a double. Because we play the percentages, we want as many darts at the double as possible. By going the T19, D12 route you are giving yourself the possibility of two darts at the double, and this is what you should do every time in those situations.

Here's how it works: You require 81 and throw the first dart at the bull. It goes into the bullseye, so you require 31. You hit the single 15 and have one dart at D8.

If your first dart hit the O/B, then you require 56. You throw for either the 16 or 20 to leave your preferred double (20 or 18 – 20 is recommended because it breaks down better). If you have breathing space, this is a great way to set up one of your favorite doubles and give yourself a good chance of winning the leg either on this visit or the next.

82
B, D16 – T14, D20

There are two different schools of thought here, and both have merits. The first is that the B, D16 route is better because if you hit the O/B you leave 57, which is a two dart out onto a good, favored double. Percentage wise it is a good choice, and is the recommended shot.

The other school of thought is that trebles are bigger than the bullseye, and we are trying to get the best odds of leaving ourselves with two darts at the double. So, in this case going for the T14, D20 may be the better shot because you have better odds of hitting T14 than you do the bullseye. The downside to this shot selection is that if you hit the single 14 then you require 68, which is 18, B or T18, D7.

Get familiar with both methods and then choose your preferred way of going for it.

83
T17, D16

There is really only one way to go for this, and it is T17, D16. Single 17 will leave 66, which is 16, B or T16, D9.

As in the finish 81 above, if your opponent is not on a finish, you have the option of going for the bull first to set up a preferred double. Bullseye leaves you 33, which is 1, D16 or 17, D8. O/B leaves you 58, which is 18, D20.

In this instance, if your opponent is not on a finish and you have the luxury of time; T17 already leaves a great double with the D16. If you hit single 17 you can set up your shot for the next turn. Single 17 will leave 66, which is either bullseye for D8, T10 for D18 or T14 for D12. If you hit the single 10, then just hit the single to set up your double – 16 for D20 or 20 for D18. On the T14, D12 shot, if you hit single 14 then go for 12 to set up D20 next time, or 20 to leave D16. If you hit the O/B going for B, D8, you will require 41, which then requires you to hit single 9 to leave D16, or 1 for D20, or even 5 for D18.

This looks complex right now on paper, but once you get practicing these finishes and going for them in different ways, you will very quickly pick it up. Allow the situation of the moment to dictate how you go for them, and make sure you choose the right combination for the right circumstances. By studying this book and practicing the lessons diligently you will have the complete finishing armory to face any situation in any game.

84
T20, D12 – T16, D18

T20, D12 is the way most people would go for this finish. As stated previously, the treble 20 is the part of the board players throw at all the time, so it makes sense to use it when it comes to sensible finishing practices. If you hit the single 20 then you are left with 64, which is 14, B, or T14, D11.

If you favor D18, then T16, D18 is your shot, and there is nothing wrong with this method. Single 16 will leave 68, which is 18, B, or T18, D7.

If you are not under immediate pressure, and have the time to set up your out-shot more carefully, then you can look at going for the bullseye with the first dart. Hitting the bullseye leaves you on 34. This is an interesting dilemma. Do you then go for it? My answer is that if you wanted to take it out in two darts then you would have gone for one of the better options described above. So, in this case, you could throw at 2, D16 with you last two darts. If you hit the O/B with the second dart, you are left with 59, which will mean 19, D20 has to be hit.

The other option here, if you have the luxury of time, would be to set up your shot if you couldn't take it out with the three darts. If you went for T20, D12, and hit single 20 with the first dart you would be left on 64. This is T16/T8 with the next dart for D16/D20. If you then hit a single 16 you would be left on 48, which is another big 16 to set up D16 next time around. Single 8 will leave 56, which is single 16 for D20 (you could set up D18 as well if that is what you wanted). The benefit of this is that it gives you three clear darts at the double on the next turn.

85
T15, D20 – T19, D14

Either of these are good ways to go for this finish. T15, D20 is the more traditional way of going for it, and if you hit single 15 you need 70, which will be 20, B, or T20, D5.

Going for T19, D14 is more unorthodox, but it is gaining in popularity as more players realize the benefit of using the trebles they throw at most frequently. D14 is a decent double because it breaks down once to D7. A single 19 leaves 66, which is 16, B, or T16, D9

This is the final finish where going for the bull with the first shot allows you to set up a double with the last dart. Bullseye leaves you with 35, which is 3, D16 or 19, D8. O/B leaves 60, which is 20, D20.

The other option here – again if you have the luxury of time – is to set up your double for the next turn and guarantee yourself three clear darts when you return. For example, single 15 leaves 70, which is T10, D20 or T18, D8. If you hit single 10 then a singe 20 sets you up nicely for D20 next time around. If you hit single 18 then a single 12 sets up D20 (or single 20 for D18).

86
T18, D16 – B, D18

T18, D16 is the way to go on 86. Single 18 will leave 68, which is 18 again for the bull. T18 with the second dart leaves D7.

If you go the bull route and hit the O/B, you are left on 61. So, throw right back at it and hit it again to leave D18. The other option is going for 15, B or T15, D8 with the last two darts.

If your second dart hits the bullseye (after the first is O/B), you are left with 11, which is a single 3 to set up D4 next time around.

If you are not under pressure, you have time to set the shot up for the next visit if you are not able to take it out on this turn. In this case, if you are going the T18, D16 route and you hit the single 18, you are left on 68. Go for T20 to leave D4, and if you hit the single 20 you require 48, which is 16/8 to set up D16/D20 next time around.

If you go for the bullseye route, and hit the O/B first dart, you could go for T15 to leave D8, and if you hit the single 15 then you are left on 46, which is 10/6 to leave D18/D20 (or you could hit single 14 to leave D16).

As mentioned though, going for it with T18, D16 is highly recommended and should be the way you go for this shot.

87
T17, D18

This is the only way to go for this finish. Single 17 will leave 70, which will be single 20, B, or T20, D5.

If you have the time, and don't need to go the bull route then you could go as follows: Single 17 will leave 70, which is T10, D20, or T18, D8. Single 10 leaves a single 20 for D20 next time around, and single 18 leaves 52, which can be done by going either 12 or 20 depending on your preferences for D20/D18.

By now, you should have a good understanding of what is left, and how to go for it when you leave the numbers from 70 and below. From now on, I will assume that you know how to go for these finishes, and I won't keep detailing them every time.

88

T20, D14 – T16, D20

This is an interesting finish in that almost every out-shot chart you see online, or that you get free with a dartboard purchase etc, tells you to go for T16, D20. Let me tell you, if you go that way when your opponent is on a finish, you are setting yourself up to lose the game.

The way to go here is T20, D14, and the reason is that if you hit the single 20 you are left with 68, which is 18, B or T18, D7. If you go for the T16, D20 route and hit the single 16, you are in a world of trouble. You then HAVE to hit either a treble/double combination or a double/double combination to win the leg, and that is far from ideal. It is certainly not playing the percentages. So, go the T20, D14 route!

If you have the time and don't need to go the bull route, then you can set yourself up on a good double when you return next time.

89

T19, D16

This is the only way to go for this shot. Single 19 will leave 70, which is taken out by going 20, B, or T20, D5.

If you have the time and don't need to go the bull route, then set yourself up for the next shot. You will be well drilled in how to get 70 by now!

90
T20, D15 – T18, D18 – B, D20

Although there are three methods mentioned here, only two are viable options for a three-dart finish. So, unless you only have two darts left, or have plenty of time to set up your finish, please discard the T18, D18 option. I only include it here for completeness. It is yet another one of the finishes you find on out-shot charts all over the world, and it will set you up for failure if you go for it with three darts in your hand.

The reason is that single 18 will leave a total of 72, which isn't a possible two dart finish without hitting a treble or two doubles. You don't want to make it any harder than it already is, so don't go for it this way.

This is another of those unusual shots where an odd double is actually the best one to go for. There aren't too many of these types of situations, but this is definitely one of them. Here's the reason: If you hit the single 20 you can still finish. It is playing the percentages. Single 20 leaves a total of 70 remaining, which as you know by now, is the highest number you can leave and still throw for a finish with two darts without hitting a treble or a double (20, B).

One other way to go for this is to go the bull route. Bullseye leaves D20, which is a great eye-catching shot, and looks great when it works. If you feel confident then this can be a good way to go, but the percentages are more in line with going the 20 route. That way, unless you miss a big single number, you are guaranteed a shot at the bullseye.

If you have 2 darts in your hand, then T18, D18 is the way to go. If you hit single 18, you will be on 72.

Chapter 4 Quiz

1. You require 81, and your opponent is sitting on 56. You throw for T19 with your first dart. What do you have left, and how are you going to go for it?
2. You require 82, and your opponent is not on a finish. You decide to go for B, D16, but your first dart misses the bull completely and lands in the single 3. What are your options at this point, and what route are you going to take? Why?
3. You require 83. Regardless of what your opponent needs, where are you going to go with your first dart? Why? What are your options if you hit the single?
4. You require 84, and your opponent is on 40. You throw for T20, D12, and hit the single 20. What do you do next? Why?
5. You require 85. What are your options with this shot, and which one do you prefer? Why?
6. You require 86, and your opponent is on 73. Which route offers you the best odds of successfully getting this out-shot? Why?
7. You require 87. Regardless of what your opponent needs, describe your shot selection. Why are you going this way? What are the advantages? What do you do if your first dart lands in the singe rather than the treble?
8. You require 88. Your opponent is on a finish. You have options here, some better than others. Which way are you going to go? Why?
9. You require 89. With your opponent sitting on 46, you instinctively know that you require T19, D16 to take the leg. Your first dart misses, and lands in T7. What do you have left, and how are you going to throw for it?
10. You require 90. With your opponent on a one dart out, what are your options? Which way gives you the best odds of taking it out? Why?

There has been a lot to learn in this chapter, and the learning curve has been pretty steep. If you take it step by step, and learn each finish one at a time, you will see the patterns forming across the dartboard and it becomes a lot easier.

The best way is to learn them whilst doing them. If you follow along in the book while practicing the finishes one at a time on the dartboard, they will quickly become engrained in your brain, and you will be surprised at how fast you pick them up.

Jim Chatterton

Chapter Five: 91-95

The finishes here are unique and deserve a special chapter of their own. By utilizing careful and clever shot utilization it is possible to take these finishes out without hitting a treble as part of the combination.

There are two distinct methods with all the finishes in this chapter (well three actually), and which way you go will depend, as always, on what your opponent requires when you walk up to take the shot.

The traditional method requires you to hit a treble as part of the combination, and is generally used when your opponent is not on a finish. The creative method doesn't require a treble, and is generally used when your opponent IS sat on a finish.

There is one more method I introduce here as well; It is another creative way of taking the finish out without having to hit a treble. It is high risk, and is only to be used in certain circumstances. But when it works, it gives a huge boost to your confidence, it's a great crowd pleaser, and it completely crushes your opponent.

I will introduce the two most conventional methods first:

Number	Solution
91	T17, D20 B, 9, D16 O/B, 16, B O/B, T16, D9
92	T20, D16 B, 10, D16 O/B, 17, B O/B, T17, D8
93	T19, D18 B, 11, D16 B, 3, D20 O/B, 18, B O/B, T18, D7
94	T18, D20 B, 12, D16 O/B, 19, B O/B, T19, D6
95	T19, D19 B, 13, D16 O/B, 20, B O/B, T20, D5

Details

As always, do the warm-up and practice sessions detailed in chapter one before moving onto the finishes.

91

T17, D20 – B, 9, D16 – O/B, 16, B – O/B, T16, D9

If your opponent is not on a finish then T17, D20 is the way to go. Single 17 leaves 74, which can be gone for in two main ways: T14, D16, or T18, D10. These can then be broken down further to set up your favored double when you return to the oche.

It gets interesting when your opponent is sat on a finish. Then what do you do? It's no good just setting up the shot for the next visit.

> *You must never assume that your opponent will miss his/her finish. You need to take the appropriate action to give yourself the best possible chance of taking it out with the three darts you have in your hands right now.*

So, your opponent is on a finish and you are facing the prospect of having to get 91 or else you will probably lose the game. Here's what you do:

You throw the first dart at the bullseye. If it goes in, then you are left with 41, which is 9, D16, or 1, D20, or 5, D18 – you get the picture. If you hit the O/B, then you are left with 66, which is single 16 for the bullseye, or T16 for D9. As long as you don't miss either the bull or the big single you are guaranteed a dart at the finish, and that is what you have to strive for every time your opponent is on a finish.

This is an advanced strategy and it is no doubt one of the more difficult ones. It only works if you put in the time and effort to practice hard, but it will pay you back time and again if you do.

92
T20, D16 – B, 10, D16 – O/B, 17, B – O/B, T17, D8

When your opponent is not on a finish, T20, D16 is the way to go for this shot. Single 20 leaves 72; which is T16, D12, T12, D18, or T20, D6. It can then be broken down further to set up a favored double when you return to the oche next time.

With your opponent on a finish, you have to try to take it out on this turn. So you throw for the bullseye with the first dart. If it goes in, you require 42, which will leave 10, D16, or 2, D20, or 6, D18. If it goes in the O/B, then you require 67, which is taken out by hitting 17, B, or T17, D8.

93
T19, D18 – B, 3, D20 – B, 11, D16 – O/B, 18, B – O/B, T18, D7

When your opponent cannot finish, the way to go is T19, D18. Single 19 leaves you on 74, which you will know intuitively by now. T14, D16, or T18, D10. It can then be broken down further to leave a favored double the next time you step to the oche.

With your opponent on a finish, you have to try to take it out on this turn. Your first dart will be at the bullseye. If it hits, will you require 43. This time I included the 3, D20 option as well as 11, D16 because some people will find 3 a better number to hit under pressure than single 11.

We have all see it on so many occasions when even the top professionals throw for single 11 and drop into single 8. If this happens, all you can do is set up the shot for your next visit and pray your opponent misses. All the good work by hitting the bull will be undone if you miss the big 11. Of course, single 3 can be missed by going either side of it, so care must be taken whichever option you decide on.

If you hit the O/B, then you will require 68, which is 18, B, or T18, D7.

94
T18, D20 – B, 12, D16 – O/B, 19, B – O/B, T19, D6

If your opponent is not on a finish then T18, D20 is the way to go. If you hit single 18, you require 76, which is T20, D8. It can then be broken down further to leave a favored double the next time you return to the oche.

If your opponent is on a finish, you have to try to take it out on this turn. Your first dart is going to be at the bullseye. If it hits, you require 44, which is 12, D16, or 4, D20, or 8, D18. If you hit the O/B, then you require 69, which is 19, B, or T19, D6.

95
T19, D19 – B, 13, D16 – O/B, 20, B – O/B, T20, D5

95 is another of those anomalies where it is best to throw for an odd double. Of course, if your opponent is not on a finish you have the luxury of refusing the D19 and setting up a better double.

This is of course down to personal preference, and when your opponent is not on a finish you can do whatever gives you the most confidence with your shot selection. Heck, you can even throw for T20, 3, D16; T18, 1, D20, or T18, 5, D18 if you have the breathing space to go for these shots. But if you have to take it out on that particular turn and you don't want to go for the bullseye, then T19, D19 is the shot to go for.

If your opponent is on a finish then you have to go for it, and the way to do that is to throw your first dart at the bullseye. If you hit it, you then require 45, which is 13, D16, 5, D20, or 9, D18. If you hit the O/B, then you require 70, which is 20, B, or T20, D5.

A third method

The three dart finishes described above that begin and end on the bullseye only work with the finishes from 91-95. The method I am about to describe likewise only has a small range that it works within, but when executed properly it is devastating – not only to watch, but also to your opponent.

> *You see it more and more with players that are experts in the art of finishing, leveraging their options and squeezing every last drop of opportunity that they possibly can.*

The method I describe here only works with finishes from 72 to 80, and it only works with even numbers, and when you have two darts in your hands. The good news is that because you always start a throw with 3 darts, the range that this method works within can be extended to as far as 140!

Here's how it works:

Let's say that you are on 93, and you have all three darts in your hands. Your opponent is on a finish and you have to take it out to win the leg. You decided to go for the bullseye first because that gives you the best percentage chance of taking the leg. However, you missed the bull completely (this happens quite often, even to the very best). Your first dart lands in the small segment of single 17.

You are now on 76, and you have to get it in two darts, or the game will most likely be over. What do you do? Well, you could go the normal way and throw for T20, D8. The trouble is that the treble is a small target, and you absolutely have to hit it or else you cannot finish. Is there a better way?

Well, actually there is, although it is by no means easy. The doubles are a bigger target than the trebles on the dartboard, and with two darts left in a do or die situation, you have to go all in or else you lose.

In our hypothetical situation presented here, you are left with 76 and have two darts in your hand. You throw the second dart and it lands right in the middle of D18. Now you take aim – and you hit the D20 smack in the middle!! For you, this is the perfect situation, and it's entirely possible if you apply yourself enough in the practice room.

Let's break it down:

I will use the finishes in the range this chapter addresses – 91 to 95 for the following examples. I will add more to it as we progress into the bigger finishes, when a big treble leaves you somewhere in the range of 72 and 80.

Please remember, your first option when going for the finishes in the 91-95 range when your opponent is on a finish should always be the bullseye route. That gives you the best possible chance of at least throwing a dart at a double to win the leg.

What I am detailing here is only when you have two darts, are left in the 72-80 range, and you simply have to hit it or you lose the leg. They are great in this range when you miss the bullseye and land in a single segment that leaves you somewhere in that range. They will come into their own as an even more viable and potent weapon in the following chapters.

91

So, you throw at the bullseye and your first dart goes into the small segment of 17. This leaves you on 74. It is too risky to throw for the T14 or T18, so you decide to go for the double/double finish. It is always good if you can throw at two familiar doubles, but that isn't always possible. So, what do you do?

You throw at D17, D20. This is a crushing blow to any opponent as they were fully expecting to get another shot. There is also something completely demoralizing to stand behind someone and watch them hit two doubles and win the game from a seemingly hopeless situation.

If you don't feel confident going the bull route, and you prefer the double/double strategy, you also have the option of going for it this way:

Start with the conventional method of T17. You hit single 17 with the first dart. Now you need 74. As above, you have the option of going for D17, D20 to crush the game.

92

Your first dart at the bullseye lands into the single 20. Now you need 72 with just two darts left in your hands.

You have two choices, and both have merits. You can throw for Double 20, D16 (or D16, D20), or you could possibly improve your odds slightly by throwing for D18 twice. If you hit the D18 with your second dart, you already have the line and the weight of shot right there, so throw for it again exactly the same way and hit it again!

The same shot could be used if you went the conventional way. Throw for T20 with the first dart. If it goes into the single, you are left with the same options as above.

In this instance, if the first dart presents itself as a good marker, then go back for T20 with the second dart. If it goes in you have scored 80 points, leaving yourself on D6 with one dart remaining.

If the first dart is blocking the treble, or it is not a good marker, then you have the option of going the double/double route, and talking the game that way.

93

Your first dart at bullseye goes into the single 19. Now you are left once again on 74. The double/double options of this are explained on finish 91 above.

In these examples, the first dart is landing in the single segment in the same manner as it would if you went the conventional way. This gives you a breakdown of the options if you prefer to take that route.

Let's say that in this instance, the first dart at bullseye lands in single 15. Now you are left with 78. You have the option of T18, D12, or, if you have no choice other than to get it on this turn, you can go for D19, D20.

94

Your first dart goes into the single 18. Now you are on 76 with two darts left. As I explained in the hypothetical example above, you go for D18, D20 and totally crush your opposition. You also have the option of going D19, D19 if you prefer. There are almost always plenty of options if you look closely enough!

95

Your first dart lands in single 19. You are now left with 76. The same applies as in finish 94 above.

I hope the above demonstrates the patterns of how these finishes work together. Once you grasp the concepts it becomes easy, and there is no further need for any mathematics.

Here's an example:

You walk to the board needing 95. Your first dart lands in single 19. You have practiced this so many times, and you understand how the patterns all work together. You don't even flinch or skip a beat because you know immediately that you now require 76. You already know what your opponent is sitting on because you looked before you walked up to throw.

So, he or she is not on a finish. You don't even have to think about it; you know the instant you saw the dart land in the single 19 that your next dart was straight at T20 for D8. Your next dart hits T5, no problem whatsoever. You automatically know that you need 61, so your third dart is thrown for the O/B, T15, or even T7.

This is how it all comes together when you apply the knowledge contained in this book, and work hard on the practice board. It is far from easy, but the rewards are worth the efforts!!

I am now going to break down all the two-dart double finishes from 72-80 so you can see how they all work together:

72 D16, D20 – D18, D18

74 D17, D20

76 D18, D20 – D19, D19

78 D19, D20

80 D20, D20

Of course, there is nothing stopping you from throwing D17, D16 when you require 66, but this goes against the percentages which we always want to keep on our side as much as possible. If you can go for a shot with a single/B, then take it. The dart odds will thank you for it later!

Chapter 5 Quiz

1. You require 91 and your opponent is sitting on 76. What is your shot selection and why?
2. You require 92 and your opponent is on a finish. You throw your first dart at the bullseye and you hit the O/B. What do you have left, and how are you going to throw for it?
3. You require 93. Your opponent is sitting on a nice two dart out. What are your options? How are you going to approach your shot selection? Why?
4. You are on 94 and your opponent is on 173. What is your shot selection? Why?
5. You are on 95. Your opponent is not on a finish. What are your options? Why? Which ones do you prefer? Why?
6. You are on 91 and your opponent is on a finish. You throw for the bullseye with your first dart and it misses, landing in the small segment of single 15. You now have two darts in your hands and you have to take it out or you lose the game. Given the situation, what options do you have with this shot? What are you going to do? Why?
7. You are on 92. Your opponent is on a finish and your first dart, thrown for the bullseye, misses and goes into the single 20. What are your options? What are you going to do? Why?
8. You are on 93 and your opponent is on 32. You throw at the bullseye and miss, landing in the single 19. What are your options? What are you going to do? Why?
9. You are on 94 and your opponent is on 40. You throw at the bullseye with your first dart and it misses, going into the single 16. What are your options? What are you going to do? Why?
10. You are on 95 and your opponent is on 24. You throw at the bull and you miss, landing in the single 15. What are your options? What are you going to do? Why?

Of course, there is always the possibility when going for the bullseye that your first dart will miss into a single that doesn't leave a finish as I explained above.

For instance, you could be on 93 and your first dart lands in the single 7. Then you are left with 86 with only two darts left. At this point you have no choice but to go for the treble/double combination finish.

Never throw in hope, but rather throw every dart with conviction and you will be amazed at how many times you can convert these finishes. Never blindly toss a dart at the board in frustration because you missed, or because you think it's over. Give every shot your full concentration and effort because it is never over until that final double has landed.

The finishes presented in this chapter are more advanced that you have seen so far. When you are left on 80 or below, which you will be on the vast majority of occasions, there are always choices with your shot selection.

Once you get above 80, not only do the shots get exponentially more difficult, but the choices become narrower, and shot selection begins to play a more crucial role.

By knowing – *and practicing* – every possible outcome beforehand, you will never be taken by surprise and will always have the answer – immediately, and without thinking – whatever the situation throws at you. And when it comes to being under pressure at the end of a game; that can often times be the difference between winning and losing.

Chapter Six: 96-100

With a few notable exceptions, the finishes presented in this chapter represent the end of the two dart finishes. Unless you utilize the double/double technique, you are forced to hit a treble as part of the combination. Only after many hours of diligent, hard practice will you be able to take these out with any regularity. But when you can, you will be joining a very exclusive group of players, and you will be a very accomplished player that is respected wherever go.

You will see, as I have mentioned previously, that the finishes form patterns and build upon each other. That concept becomes very evident from now onwards as you see finish after finish that is built upon the ones you studied previously. Once you realize that, it strips away the mystique of the higher, seemingly impossible finishes and breaks them down into achievable, understandable, less intimidating finishes. In short, it gives you the confidence to hit them!!

Number	Solution
96	T20, D18
97	T19, D20
98	T20, D19
99	T19, 10, D16 T17, 16, D16
100	T20, D20

Details

96

T20, D18

There is really only one way to go for this, and it is T20, D18. If you hit the single 20 you are left with 76. This is where you can see how the finishes build up on top of previous ones, so you instinctively know what to go for when you are on 76. The big difference is that you only have two darts in which to get it, not the three you had earlier in the book. And this makes a massive difference.

As always, it depends on what score your opponent has left when you step up to throw for the 96. If you hit single 20, then as stated you are left with 76. Now, here is another interesting concept: If your first dart is a great marker for the second — and by that, I mean if it is just above (or below) the treble and is inviting the second dart to nudge it and go into the treble, then stay where you are and throw at it again. If it works, and it goes in, then you are on D8 and you have set up a great finish under pressure.

This also works if you like to "under stack" as the late, great Sid Waddell used to say. Which means that if you like to stack your darts on top of each other, and your first dart is perfectly placed to stack the second dart into the treble, then stay there and go for it again. As always, keep the percentages on your side as much as you possibly can. It will reward you many times over.

If your first dart in the single 20 offers no marker for the second dart, then you have a choice to make. You could readjust and throw for the T20 again, or you could utilize the double/double technique. In this situation, the doubles are larger than the trebles, and it gives you a bigger target to aim at. So here you could go for D18, D20 to win the game and demoralize your opponent.

Of course, the big danger with going for the double/double is missing the board completely with the second dart. This is the chance you take. These shots are high risk/high reward.

With your opponent sat on a good finish, you are in a do or die situation, and it is all or nothing when you throw at the finish. So, it makes sense to throw for the biggest target you possibly can that will give you the best possible odds of winning the leg. Not to mention the boost of raw confidence it gives you when you successfully take out a shot like this.

If your opponent is not on a finish, then you can afford to take your time and set the shot up for the next turn. If you hit single 20, and then a second single 20, you can then throw for a single 16 to leave D20, or 20 again for D18 next time around. You will possess the expert knowledge to know when to change the shot selection to suit the situation, and that makes a huge difference to your game.

97

T19, D20

There is only one way to go for this, and it is T19, D20. If you hit the single 19 then you are left with 78, and you already know what this is without even thinking about it.

If your opponent is on a finish, then you have the option of going for the double/double finish of D19, D20, which is a grandstand finish.

However, there is a big difference between grandstanding and pragmatism, and when you are in the situation of having to hit the finish or risk losing the game; it becomes a sensible way to go for it.

If your opponent is not on a finish, then you can go for T18, D12 with your second and third darts. But you already knew that!

98
T20, D19

This is another of those unorthodox finishes where an odd double is the recommended way to go for the out-shot. This is because there is no other treble/double combination that works with 2 darts, so this is the only sensible way to go for this shot.

T16, B is a mathematically possible out-shot, but with 3 darts in your hands, it goes against all the principles of this method and should be discounted.

If your opponent is on a good finish and your first dart lands in the single 20, you will be left with 78. This gives you the option of throwing for D19, D20 and taking the game.

If your opponent is not on a finish then you will be able to go for T18, D12 if your first dart lands in the singe 20.

99
T19, 10, D16 – T17, 16, D16

This is the first of the three dart finishes. It cannot be taken out with two darts, so avoid leaving 99 if at all possible. The recommended shot is going for T19 first. This leaves 42, which can be taken out a number of ways.

The other way that more and more players are going for is to go for T17 with the first dart. This leaves 48, which is a great two dart finish.

The reason that the T19 route is recommended over the T17 is because of what the single number leaves if you miss the treble. Single 19 leaves 80, which can be done with double 20/double 20. Even if your opponent is not on a finish, leaving 80 is still recommended because all it takes is two single 20's to guarantee yourself three clear darts at a double on your next turn.

You also have the option of going for T16, D16 when you are on 80 with two darts left.

If you go the T17 route and hit the single, you are left with 82. You are then forced to hit the bullseye or T14 if you want to take the shot out on this turn. Both of these options are difficult, especially under pressure. The 17 route is not the recommended way to go.

If your opponent is not on a finish and you hit single 17, then hitting the O/B, single 17 again will leave D20 next time around.

100

T20, D20

Again, there is only one real way to go for this finish, and that is T20, D20. If you are doing an exhibition, or showing your new-found skills off to your friends, you can go for B, B, otherwise, this shot is always T20, D20

If you hit the single 20, you are in the same situation as you were in finish 96 above. If the first dart is a good marker for the second dart, then by all means go right back at it for T20, D10. If your first dart blocks the treble, or if it isn't a good marker, then you have the option of D20/D20. You will see many players take out 100 this way in a close contest.

Another way of going for this shot if your first dart goes into the single 20 and blocks the treble bed, is to go for T16, D16. It is far better to go for 80 in this manner with two darts in your hands as opposed to having all three. If your opponent is on a finish, then this is a good alternative to the double/double option. If your opponent is not on a finish, then you have the luxury of trying to set it up for the next turn if your second dart hits single 16.

Chapter 6 Quiz

1. You require 96, and your opponent is on 48. Your first dart goes into the single 20, landing right above the treble, giving you a great marker dart. What are your options? Which way are you going to go? Why?
2. You require 96, and your opponent is on 48. Your first dart lands high in the treble 20, giving you no marker to aim at. Where are you going to go with the second dart? Why?
3. You require 97. Your opponent is not on a finish. Your first dart goes into single 19. What are your options? Which way are you going to go with the remaining two darts? Why?
4. You require 97. Your opponent is on 56. Your first dart goes into single 19. What are you left with? Which way are you going to go for it? Why?
5. You require 98, and your opponent is on 32. Why is this finish unusual? What is the best way to go for it? Why?
6. You require 98, and your opponent is not on a finish. Your first dart goes into the T20. What are your options at this point? What are you going to do? Why?
7. You require 99, and your opponent is on 78. Why is leaving 99 a bad choice? What are your options? How are you going to go for this? Why?
8. You are on 99, and your opponent is on 36. Your first dart lands in the single 19. What are your options at this point? How are you going to go for it? Why?
9. You are on 100, and your opponent is on 86. The first dart lands just above the treble 20 wire, giving you a great marker; what are your options in this scenario? What are you going to do? Why?
10. You are on 100, and your opponent is on 40. Your first dart lands just above the treble 20 wire, blocking the treble bed; what are your options at this point? What are you going to do? Why?

There is no doubt that the finishes presented here are very difficult, and they just keep getting harder and harder as we progress. If you have worked diligently throughout the chapters presented so far, you will have ingrained the finishing patterns deep into your brain, which is half the battle when it comes to being a great finisher.

The other half – *the most difficult half by a long way* – is being able to actually hit them with any semblance of consistency. Please remember, even the very best players don't even come close to taking these kinds of finishes out every time. Nobody does.

Keep practicing as hard as you can, and you will be surprised at how your knowledge and skills will improve. You will take great satisfaction from all the effort you put into it at home - behind the scenes - when you take out that 100+ finish in the final leg of a high quality, very close match. Your confidence will soar (another hugely important aspect of this game), and you will realize that all the hard work and dedication is paying off.

You will realize that you really can play this game to a high level and compete with the best players in your area and beyond. The hard work you put in now will pay you back many times over further down the road, so don't give up and keep going. We're now entering the realm of the big 100+ glamour finishes!!

Jim Chatterton

Chapter Seven: 101-120

We are now entering the world of the big finishes, the ones that everyone dreams of taking out at a crucial point in a match. Because you have worked hard to even get to this point, you will find the finishes in the 100-120 range are not as hard as they first appeared, and you will be confident of hitting them every time you step up to the board. Or at least you will be confident setting them up for a one dart finish on the next turn.

With four notable exceptions, all these are now three dart finishes, so shot selection at this point is crucial.

Number	Solution
101	T19, 12, D16
	19, B, D16
	19, T14, D20
	T20, 9, D16
	T20, 1, D20
	20, T19, D12
	T17, B
102	T20, 10, D16
	T20, 2, D20
	20, B, D16
	20, T14, D20
103	T20, 3, D20
	T20, 11, D16
	20, T17, D16
	T19, 14, D16

	T19, 6, D20 T19, 10, D18 19, T20, D12 19, T16, D18
104	T20, 12, D16 T20, 4, D20 20, T20, D12 20, T16, D18 T18, 18, D16 T16, 16, D20 T18, B
105	T19, 16, D16 T19, 8, D20 19, T18, D16 T20, 13, D16 T20, 5, D20 20, T15, D20 20, T19, D14
106	T20, 14, D16 T20, 6, D20 T20, 10, D18 20, T18, D16
107	T19, 18, D16 T19, 10, D20 19, T20, D14 19, T16, D20 T19, B T20, 15, D16 T20, 7, D20 20, T17, D18

108	T20,16, D16
	T20, 8, D20
	20, T20, D14
	20, T16, D20
	T19, 19, D16
	T18, 18, D18
	T17, 17, D20
109	T20, 17, D16
	T20, 9, D20
	20, T19, D16
	T19, 20, D16
	T19, 12, D20
	19, T18, D18
	19, B, D20
110	T20, 18, D16
	T20, 10, D20
	20, T18, D18
	20, T20, D15
	20, B, D20
	T20, B
111	T20, 19, D16
	T20, 11, D20
	20, T17, D20
	T19, 14, D20
	T19, 18, D18
	19, T20, D16
112	T20, 20, D16
	T20, 12, D20
	T18, 18, D20
113	T20, 13, D20

	T20, 17, D18 20, T19, D18 T19, 16, D20 T19, 20, D18 19, T18, D20
114	T20, 14, D20 T20, 18, D18 20, T18, D20 T18, 20, D20 18, T20, D18
115	T19, 18, D20 19, T20, D18 T20, 15, D20 20, T19, D19
116	T20, 16, D20 T20, 20, D18 T19, 19, D20
117	T20, 17, D20 20, T19, D20 T19, 20, D20 19, T20, D19
118	T20, 18, D20 20, T20, D19
119	T19, T10, D16 T19, T14, D10 T19, 12, B T19, T12, D13 19, T20, D20

120	T20, 20, D20

Details

101

T19, 12, D16 – 19, B, D16 – 19, T14, D20 – T20, 9, D16 - T20, 1, D20

20, T19, D12 – T17, B

As you can see, there are lots of choices in this range!! In fact, I have only included the ones that are recommended the most. There are countless other ways to get these finishes, but these are the ones that keep the percentages on your side, which is one of the golden rules of this book.

Whether to start this combination with T20 or T19 is a personal choice. The only benefit of starting with T19 is that it leaves you a shot at the bullseye to leave D16, or hitting the O/B to leave 57, which is a simple singe 17 to leave D20 next turn (if you get one, depending what your opponent is on).

The only time you need to go for T17, B is when you have two darts in your hands and your opponent is on a finish. This comes more into play in the next chapter when we get into the finishes in the 121-130 range. Otherwise, always go for it in one of the ways described above.

I won't break down the finishes in great detail, explaining what to go for if you miss the treble with the first two darts, because by now you will have this down without even thinking about it. It's just a simple matter of remembering the patterns, and by doing this it keeps the mathematics down to a bare minimum, and when you have practiced these for a while even the need for basic math goes away – you just know what to throw for without even thinking about it. It becomes as instinctive as putting on your favorite pair of slippers.

102
T20, 10, D16 – T20, 2, D20 – 20, B, D16 – 20, T14, D20

Treble 20 is the way to start this combination, and from there you have several choices depending on your preferences. It's worth noting that even if you miss either side of the 20 with the first dart, you still are able to finish the combination.

If you drift into the T5, you need 87. Single 5 leaves you on 97, and single 1 leaves you with 101. The only one to avoid is T1 as this leaves 99, which cannot be taken out in two darts.

103
T20, 3, D20 – T20, 11, D16 – 20, T17, D16 – T19, 14, D16 – T19, 6, D20
T19, 10, D18 - 19, T20, D12 – 19, T16, D18

Again, there are lots of choices here. Whether to start with T19 or T20 is a personal choice as one doesn't give any advantage over the other.

It may seem more symmetrical to start with an odd double on an odd numbered finish, and there is logic to that. Be aware, however, that this is not always the case. As you will see when we get into the next chapter, there certainly are exceptions to this rule!

104
T20, 12, D16 – T20, 4, D20 – 20, T20, D12 – 20, T16, D18
T18, 18, D16 – T16, 16, D20 – T18, B

More and more, players are starting to throw for a treble/single of the same number to leave a preferred double. This makes sense in that you already have your line of sight and weight of shot set up for one particular number, so it pays to stay there for the second dart before moving onto the double.

With this finish, you get that option with both the 18's and the 16's. Going the way of the 18's, you get two darts at the treble before moving onto D16, and with the 16's you get two darts at the treble before moving onto the D20. This comes down to which double you favor.

Most players will still choose to go the more traditional ways though, and the T20 route will always be a great way to start this combination. Just know that you have choices, and find your own preference.

The T18, B route is only to be used when you have two darts in your hands and your opponent is on a double.

105
T19, 16, D16 – T19, 8, D20 – 19, T18, D16 – T20, 13, D16 T20, 5, D20 – 20, T15, D20 – 20, T19, D14

There are other ways to approach this finish, such as T15, 20, D20, but as always, you need to keep the odds on your side as much as possible, and the big trebles of 20, 19 and 18 are the ones that are thrown at the most frequently.

Starting with T19 on this combination probably makes the most sense, but there are plenty of players that would argue against that. Practice them all, get to know them all so you know your options, and then find your favorite way to go for it.

The benefit from starting on the 20's, is that a miss either side still leaves a finish. For example, 5, T20, D20 and 1, T18, B.

106
T20, 14, D16 – T20, 6, D20 – T20, 10, D18 – 20, T18, D16

T20 is the way to start this combination. If you hit it, then you have your choice of double to leave depending on your preferences. If you hit the single, then T18, D16 is the shot to take on.

You could, of course, go for B, D18 with 86 left, but the odds are better if you go for the T18 instead of the bullseye.

107

T19, 18, D16 – T19, 10, D20 – T19, B – 19, T20, D14
9, T16, D20 – T20, 15, D16 – T20, 7, D20 – 20, T17, D18

T19 is the obvious way to go for this shot. If you hit the single 19, then you have options on 88. With just two darts in your hands, T16, D20 is a good shot to go for. More and more players are going back up for T20, D14 as they throw at the T20 more than anything else.

T19, B is only to be used when you have two darts in your hands and your opponent is on a finish.

There is nothing wrong with starting the combination on T20, but you will find that the vast majority of players start on the T19. There is a better symmetry by going for it in this manner.

108

T20, 16, D16 – T20, 8, D20 – 20, T20, D14 – 20, T16, D20
T19, 19, D16 – T18, 18, D18 – T17, 17, D20

This finish gives you a plethora of good options. You can set up your shot to throw for your favorite double. You can start the combination on T20, and then throw for a different single to set up your desired double.

More and more, players are throwing for a treble/single combination on the same number to set up a good double. This makes a lot of sense because you already have your sights set on one particular area of the board. If you hit it, there is little adjustment required to hit it again, and certainly less than there is when you are moving around the board throwing at different numbers.

Finishing is difficult enough as it is, so when the board offers you a helping hand with some good natural advantages go ahead and take it.

109

T20, 17, D16 – T20, 9, D20 – 20, T19, D16 – T19, 20, D16

T19, 12, D20 – 19, T18, D18 – 19, B, D20

Either treble is good for starting this combination. Neither gives any advantage over the other, so choose your favored method and go for it!!

110

T20, 18, D16 – T20, 10, D20 – 20, T18, D18 – 20, T20, D15

20, B, D20 – T20, B

Obviously T20 is the way to start this combination. If you hit it, you have good options available to set up your preferred double.

The interesting part about this finish is the options you have if your first dart lands in the single 20. Depending on what score your opponent needs, this is a good example of where an odd double may be the preferred way to go for it.

If your opponent is on a good finish, and you simply have to get it or face defeat, throw your first dart as usual at T20. If it goes high (or low), and presents itself as a good marker for the second dart, then go right back at it for the T20.

If it goes in, then you have one dart at the D15. This may not be an ideal double, but you only have one shot at taking this out, so use the advantages your darts and the dartboard give to you. If you only have one dart at a double to win a match, then it doesn't matter which one it is. They are all the same size, and you have practiced them all. So, you can hit them all.

If your first dart is a blocker dart, or you have more time to set it up – or if you just fancy it more – then you can always throw for the T18, D18 if your first dart is in single 20. Or even B, D20. These are all good shots, just be aware of your options and choose accordingly.

111

T20, 19, D16 – T20, 11, D20 – 20, T17, D20 – T19, 14, D20 T19, 18, D18 – 19, T20, D16

Starting with either T20 or T19 is good with this shot. Neither gives any advantages over the other, so as stated above, be aware of your options and choose accordingly.

112

T20, 20, D16 – T20, 12, D20 – T18, 18, D20

T20 would be the obvious choice to start the combination with this finish unless your favored double is D20 and you prefer to leave it above all others whenever you can. In that case, the T18 route may be the way to go because you have the treble and single 18 to throw for, giving you some margin of error with your first two darts.

If you are a devout D16 hitter – and the vast majority of players are – then the T20 is definitely the way to start the combination.

113

T20, 13, D20 – T20, 17, D18 – 20, T19, D18 – T19, 16, D20 T19, 20, D18 – 19, T18, D20

As above, either of these trebles is a good way to start the combination. The majority of players start with the T20, and this is the recommended route. But either is fine.

114

T20, 14, D20 – T20, 18, D18 – 20, T18, D20 – T18, 20, D20

18, T20, D18

T20 is the recommended way to start this combination. There is no advantage in going with the T18 with the first dart. It is presented here to demonstrate that there are always options, but in this case T20 is the way to go.

115

T19, 18, D20 – 19, T20, D18 – T20, 15, D20 – 20, T19, D19

T19 is the way to start this combination. The reason is that if you miss it, you have better set up options than if you started with T20.

If you hit single 19, you then require 96, which is T20, D18. This is a much better option than if you had started on T20, because that leaves 95, which with two darts is T19, D19. Always go for the shot that gives you the best odds of getting it.

There are other ways of going for this finish, such as 20, T15, B, or B, O/B, D20. These are not recommended ways to go for this, but it is always good to be aware of the other options. The bullseye route is a great exhibition shot!

116

T20, 16, D20 – T20, 20, D18 – T19, 19, D20

Starting with the T19 has a lot of merit with this finish. You have two shots at 19, and then you will have a dart at D20. The same can be said about starting on D20, because if you hit the single with the first dart, you then have another go at it to leave D18. So, either way is good. As always, know your options and choose accordingly.

117

T20, 17, D20 – 20, T19, D20 – T19, 20, D20 – 19, T20, D19

T20 is the way to begin this combination. This is because of the finish that is left if you hit the single number.

If you hit single 20, you are left with 97, which is T19, D20. If you hit single 19, you are left with a much less desirable finish in T20, D19. So, start this combination with the T20

118

T20, 18, D20 – 20, T20, D19

T20 is the way to start this combination. If you hit the single then you require 98, which with two darts will be T20, D19.

You could start the combination on the 18's, but this is not recommended. If you hit the treble with the first dart, then you are still left with 64, which with two darts will be taken out by hitting 14, B (or T14, D11). This is far from ideal.

If you hit the single 18 with the first dart, you would be left with 100, which is T20, D20, but again this isn't recommended because you never want to throw for a single with the first dart in a three-dart combination. You want to have two darts to hit the treble, and one for the double. Otherwise the odds are stacked too high against you.

119

T19, T10, D16 – T19, T14, D10 - T19, 12, B
T19, T12, D13 - 19, T20, D20

In the finish above (118), I stated that it is far from ideal to go for a treble with the first dart that didn't leave you on 60 or below. And yet on this finish, I am going to completely contradict myself and state that the recommended method of starting this combination – indeed the only way to start this combination is to go for the T19 with the first dart.

If you start with the T20 then you will be left with 59, which leaves you below the magic threshold of 60 with two darts remaining. So why isn't this recommended? The answer is that it goes completely against the percentages, and therefore the methods taught in this book. If you hit the single 20 with your first dart, you are left on 99, which is not a two-dart finish. And that is a no-no.

So, you always start this combination with the lesser of the two evils – T19. If you hit it, then you are on 62. If your opponent is on a finish, you will go for 12, B (or T12, D13).

If your opponent is not on a finish, then you have more time to set up the shot. In this case you could go for T10, D16, or T14, D10, or T18, D4. If you hit the single 19 (and many times you will), it leaves a good shot at T20, D20.

120

T20, 20, D20

There is only one way to go for this finish, and that is the "shanghai" shot on the 20's - T20, 20, D20. This is a favored finish of many of the top professional players, and they hit it with a great degree of accuracy.

Chapter 7 Quiz

1. You require 101 and your opponent is sitting on 67. What is your shot selection going to be? Why?
2. You require 105. Your opponent is not on a finish. Your first dart goes into single 19. What are your options with the last two darts? What are you going to throw for? Why?
3. You require 107. Your opponent is sitting on D20. You throw for the T19 first dart and hit it. What are you going to do next? Why?
4. You require 108. You have plenty of options with this out-shot. Which way are you going to go? Why?
5. You are on 110. Your opponent is on 73. You throw your first dart at T20, and it goes to the right, landing in T1. What are your options with the last two darts? What is your shot selection going to be? Why?
6. You require 110. Your opponent is on a good finish. You throw the first dart at T20, and it lands in the single 20, just above the wire. What are your options with this shot? What is your shot selection going to be? Why?
7. You are on 112. Your opponent is on 84. You throw for the T20, and drift into the single 5. What are your options with the last two darts? What are you going to do? Why?
8. You are on 113. Regardless of where your opponent is sitting, what are your options on this out-shot? Which way would you go for it? Why?
9. You are on 116. Your opponent is on a finish. What are your options with this shot? Which way are you going to go for it? Why?
10. You are on 119. Your opponent is on a good finish. You need a good, careful shot selection with this one. What is your shot selection? Why?

There are many ways of getting the finishes in this chapter. The trick is to always choose the best shot that gives you the best odds of success in any particular situation.

For instance, if you are on 119 and your opponent is sitting on a good finish, then the shot selection would be T19, 12, B (or T12, D13, but be careful with these shots because the area around the treble is smaller, and there is a possibility you will miss the number completely).

However, if your opponent is not on a finish, then going that way is probably not the best solution (although it always looks good when they go in). In this instance, if you hit the T19 with the first dart, you would be better served going for a treble/double combination such as T10/D16. If you hit the single 10, you could use the last dart to set up your double for the next turn, thus guaranteeing yourself three clear darts at a double.

Players have been seen throwing for the bullseye with the first dart on these out-shots. I have deliberately omitted them from the chart and details above because it is not a good way to go for them.

Here's why:

Let's say you are on 101, which is the lowest number in this chapter. With three darts in your hands, you decide to throw for the bullseye with the first dart. So, you hit the middle red bit. You then need 51, which is a good two dart out.

Unless you are a player of the caliber of Michael van Gerwen or Gary Anderson, the chances are you will not hit the bullseye very often with that first dart, so the best you can hope for is to hit the O/B. This changes the outlook completely.

You are now on 76, and have only two darts left in your hands. Assuming your opponent is on a finish, you have to get it or risk losing. What are your options? Well, you have T20, D8, or D18, D20 as two good options.

If you look closer at this, you will see that going for the bullseye did not give you any advantages at all. You still need a treble/double (or two doubles) combination even after hitting the O/B. If you hit the T19 first dart, you need a much easier single/double out-shot. Even if you hit the single you are no worse off than you were by going for the bullseye with the first dart.

When going for the finishes with three darts, unless otherwise stated, use the trebles with higher values (20-17) whenever possible. It increases your odds of success and keeps them on your side. There are occasions when it is preferable to choose the bull over a big treble, and these are dealt with as they arise.

Chapter Eight: 121-130

The bullseye plays a prominent role in the finishes detailed in this chapter. As you will see, shot selection plays a crucial part in setting these up, and the odds of making the shot will turn in your favor when you know how to do it. And of course, they feel great when they go in!!

Number	Solution
121	T20, 11, B
	T20, T11, D14
	20, T17, B
	T17, 20, B
	T17, T20, D5
	17, T18, B
	T20, O/B, D18
	T20, T15, D8
	T17, T18, D8
	T17, T10, D20
	B, T13, D16
	O/B, T20, D18
122	T18, 18, B
	T18, T18, D7
123	T19, 16, B
	T19, T16, D9
	19, T18, B

124	T20, 14, B
	T20, T14, D11
	20, T18, B
125	O/B, T20, D20
	B, T17, D12
	B, O/B, B
	T15, D20, D20
	15, T20, B
126	T19, 19, B
	T19, T19, D6
127	T20, 17, B
	T20, T17, D8
	20, T19, B
128	T18, T18, D10
	T18, T14, D16
	18, T20, B
129	T19, T16, D12
	T19, T12, D18
	T19, T20, D6
	T19, D16, D20
	T19, D18, D18
	19, T20, B
130	T20, T20, D5
	T20, 20, B

Details

121

Lots of options – see above chart

As you can see from the above chart, there are lots of options for this finish, and these are just a few of the possible combinations!

However, don't get despondent. As I will explain, the choices break down logically to a few small groups, and when you think of it in this way it becomes much easier to grasp.

There are three main schools of thought with this finish – using the T20, T17, or the bullseye. Dutch players, especially Raymond van Barneveld, seem to like throwing for the bullseye first with this shot, although they are in the minority. Other notary players such as Robert Thornton like to throw for T17 first. The great Eric Bristow used to always go for T17 with his first dart. The vast majority of players throw for the T20 with their first dart though, and this is where I suggest you start when you are studying this finish.

Unless you are a very accomplished player like Raymond van Barneveld, going for the bullseye first is not a good percentage shot. If you hit the bullseye, which is a great shot, you still have to hit a treble/double combination to finish the shot (T13, D16, or T17, D10). You are much more likely to hit the O/B, which leaves you on 96. This is still a treble/double combination, and it is for this reason that this method is not recommended, especially when you are first starting out.

As stated above, the vast majority of players throw for 121 by starting on the 20. If you hit the treble, you are then on 61. Assuming that your opponent is on a finish, then the shot will be 11, B (or T11, D14).

If you hit the single 20, you will require 101, which with two darts left and your opponent on a finish, is T17, B

If you decide to start with the 17, then if you hit the treble it is the same as above just in reverse, which is T17, 20, B. You can aim at the T20 as well, and if you hit it you will be on D5. If you hit the single, you then require 104, which with two darts and your opponent on a double will be completed by hitting T18, B.

If your opponent is not on a finish, then you have a license to set up the shots in a more preferable manner. For instance, if you go T20 first dart and hit it, you then need 61. This can be O/B, D18, or T15, D8, or even T7, D20 if that is what you prefer.

If you hit T17 with the first dart, you will require 70. This can be taken out with T10, D20, T18, D8, or 20, B.

Whichever method you decide to take, always be aware of what score your opponent is on before you step up to the oche. That way you will always be able to make the right shot selection.

122
T18, 18, B – T18, T18, D7 – O/B, T19, D20

When your opponent is on a finish, going for the 18's is the way to go for this shot. You have two chances to hit the treble, and the treble/single leaves the bullseye.

If your first dart goes into the treble, go right back for it again to leave D7. Just be careful that you don't miss the big number completely and mess up the good work you did with the first dart when you hit the treble 18.

Another plus from going this way, is that if your first dart goes low and hits the T4, will be left with 110, which can still be taken out with two darts – T20, B.

How To Master The Art Of Finishing

If your opponent is not on a finish, then you have free reign to set it up in any way you prefer. For instance, you can go for T20 with the first dart. T20 leaves 62. Single 20 leaves 102, which is T20 again to leave 42 with one dart, so you can set it up for the next turn.

Going for the bullseye with the first dart can be a good choice if you are not under pressure. If you hit it, you will require 72 with two darts remaining. You have several options with this.

If the first dart is O/B, try to follow it up with T19, D20, which is a brilliant way to take out 122.

When your opponent is on a finish, the only way to go for this is to start with the 18's.

123
T19, 16, B – T19, T16, D9 – 19, T18, B

When your opponent is on a finish always start this combination on the 19's. If you hit it, you will be left with 66, which is 16, B, or T16, D9. If you hit the single, you are left with 104, which you can still finish with two darts – T18, B.

If your opponent is not on a finish, then you can set it up as you like. T19 leaves 66, which could be T10, D18, or B, D8, or T14, D12. You could even go for the T20 first dart, but for this shot T19 is the recommended way to start the combination, no matter what your opponent requires.

124
T20, 14, B – T20, T14, D11 – 20, T18, B

This combination should be started on the 20. Hit the treble and you need 64, which with two darts in your hands and your opponent on a finish is 14, B, or T14, D11. If you hit the single 20 then you can still finish by going for the T18, B.

If your opponent is not on a finish, you can set it up however you prefer. If you hit T20 first dart, then with 64 remaining you could throw for T16/T8 to leave D16/D20.

125
O/B, T20, D20 – B, T17, D12 – B, O/B, B – 15, T20, B T15, D20, D20

The vast majority of players go for this combination by starting on the bullseye. This is one of those times when going for the bullseye first makes sense and puts the odds in your favor.

If you hit the O/B, you are left with a good T20/D20 combination to make the finish.

If you hit the bullseye, you are left with 75. If your opponent is on a finish you have to weigh up your options. If the first dart is blocking the bullseye and makes hitting it a second time extremely difficult and unlikely, then throw for the T17/D12 combination.

If the bullseye shot is a good marker to slide another one alongside it, throw at the O/B and bullseye again. This could be seen as showboating, and it is a glamour shot for sure, but in this situation, when you absolutely have to get it or lose, it makes sense if your first dart is a good guide for another to go alongside it.

Double World Match-play champion Rod Harrington used to always go for T15, D20, and D20 with this shot when his opponents were on a finish. He even did it in the final of the World Match-play against Ronnie Baxter. It is a good percentage shot to be sure, and you have the added advantage of leaving the option of T20/B if your first dart hits the single 15. But the majority of players go for the O/B, T20, D20 combination with this shot, and this is the recommended way to go for it.

If your opponent is not on a finish then you have more time to get the finish, but on this occasion, it is still advisable to go for the bullseye with the first dart. If you hit the O/B, you are left with a great chance of taking it out on this turn, and that is always a good thing when you can do it.

126

T19, 19, B – T19, T19, D6

This combination should be started on the 19's. You have two shots at the treble in order to leave the bullseye. If you hit the treble with the first dart, go right back at it again for D6.

Naturally, if your opponent is not on a finish then you don't need to go for it this way. T20 leaves 66, which has plenty of options available. Single 20 leaves 106, which means you throw at T20 again to leave 46, which is a simple setup for the next turn. If you hit two single 20's, then you are left with 86, which is a dart at T18 for D16.

127

T20, 17, B – T20, T17, D8 – 20, T19, B

Even though this is an odd number, this is one of those times that you start it on the 20 bed. The reason is that even if you hit a single 20 with the first dart, you can still finish the shot. If you went for 19 with the first dart and hit the single, then you wouldn't be able to finish.

If the first dart goes in the T20, then you throw for 67 in the conventional manner – T17, D8. This has the added safety net of leaving the bullseye if you hit the single 17.

There is also the option of starting this shot on T17, which is the same as above only reversed. If you hit T17 with the first dart, you are left with 76, which is either a treble/double or double/double combination. Single 17 will leave 110, which is T20, B

With your opponent on a double, there is no advantage to hitting the T17 with the first dart, as it still leaves you needing another treble before you reach a double, whereas if you hit T20 with the first dart, you are left with 67, which is a much better leave in these circumstances.

This is the reason why starting on the T20 is the recommended way to go.

128
18, T20, B – T18, T18, D10 – T18, T14, D16

This shot has to be started on the 18 bed. If you went for the 20 with the first dart and hit the single, you would not be able to finish. If you hit single 18, then it is T20, B.

If you hit the treble, then you are on 74. Because you have already hit the treble, and your aim and weight of shot are right where you aimed it, it makes sense to throw right back for the T18 again with the second dart. If you hit it, you are on D10. If you hit the single then you are left with 56, which will have to be set up for the next turn in the hope that you get a shot at it.

You also have the option of throwing for T14, D16 if the first dart goes into the T18. If the treble is blocked from the first dart, or if you just prefer going the T14 route, then go ahead and throw for it. But the odds are probably better if the first dart goes into the T18 and you throw right back at it again for D10. Matches are won and lost on fine margins, so keep the odds on your side as much as you possibly can.

129
T19, T16, D12 – T19, T12, D18 – T19, T20, D6 – 19, T20, B
T19, D16, D20 – T19, D18, D18

Whichever way you eventually decide to go for this shot, you always start out on the 19's. If you hit the treble, then you have plenty of options. T16 leaves D12, or T12 leaves D18, or even T20 leaves D6.

The doubles are bigger than the trebles, and if your opponent is on an easy finish, it may be beneficial to go for it this way. Remember, it is okay if you try for these finishes and fail. At least you lost trying, and you can take the positives out of the situation whatever the outcome.

If you decide to go the double/double route, then D16 leaves D20, or D18 leaves the same thing again – D18. If you get one there is a good likelihood that you will get it again, and it is for this reason that going the D18/D18 is probably the best way to go for this type of shot.

If you hit the single 19 first then you can still finish by going T20, B

130
T20, 20, B – T20, T20, D5

This is a nice out-shot to take on as it gives you two chances at the big T20, and if you hit one of them and keep the other dart in the single 20, you have a shot at the bull for the game. Many a big match has been won with this finish.

Of course, if your opponent is not on a finish, then you have plenty of options. Still start the shot on T20, and if you hit it, you are left with 70. From there you have options to setup your preferred double.

If you hit the single 20, you are left with 110, which is T20 again. This time, however, because your opponent is not on a finish, you don't throw at the bullseye (unless you want to). Instead, you set up your favorite double for the next turn when you will have three clear darts to take it out.

If you hit two single 20's with the first two darts, you are on 90. You could throw for the T18 to leave 36, or you could throw for the bullseye to leave 40. Either is a good option.

Chapter 8 Quiz

1. You require 121. Your opponent is on a finish. What are your options with this out-shot? How are you going to go for it? Why?
2. You require 122. With your opponent on a finish, where are you going to start this combination? Why? What do you do if you hit the single? What do you do if you hit the treble?
3. You require 123. Your opponent is on 89. What is your shot selection with this finish? Why? What do you do next if you hit the single with the first dart?
4. You require 124. Your opponent is on 24. What is your shot selection with this out-shot? Why? What do you do next if the first dart goes into the treble?
5. You require 125. Your opponent is on 72. What are your options with this out-shot? How are you going to go for it? Why?
6. You require 126. With your opponent on a finish, where are you going to start this combination? Why? What do you do if you hit the single? What do you do if you hit the treble?
7. You require 127. With your opponent on a finish, where are you going to start this combination? Why? What do you do if you hit the single? What do you do if you hit the treble?
8. You require 128. Your opponent is on 64. Where are you going to start this combination? Why? What are your options if you hit the treble with the first dart? Which way would you then go for it? Why?

9. You require 129. Your opponent is 68. How are you going to approach this finish? Why? What will you do if you hit the treble with the first dart? Why?
10. You require 130. Your opponent is on 42. What are you going to do? Why?

Hopefully by now you have seen how these finishes work together in patterns that flow together and make it easier to remember them. Make the dartboard work for you and your finishing will improve tremendously. With plenty of practice and the right mindset, finishing can become the strong point of your game, and if this happens you will be a fearsome player that everybody respects and admires.

Jim Chatterton

Chapter Nine: 131-140

You have now reached the area of the glamorous, super finishes. These are the ones that every dart player dreams of getting in a tight match to win the game.

The finishes in this chapter all require a combination of two trebles and a double to complete them, which leaves no room for error. However, with some creative shot selections, it is possible to hit some of them by only hitting one treble.

Number	Solution
131	T20, T13, D16 T20, T17, D10 T17, D20, D20
132	B, B, D16 B, T14, D20 O/B, T19, B
133	T20, T19, D8 T19, D19, D19
134	T20, T14, D16 T20, T18, D10 T18, D20, D20
135	B, T15, D20 B, T19, D14 O/B, T20, B

	T19, T18, D12
136	T20, T20, D8
	T16, T16, D20
137	T20, T19, D10
	T19, T16, D16
	T19, D20, D20
138	T20, T18, D12
	T19, T19, D12
	T20, T20, D9
139	T20, T13, D20
	T20, T19, D11
	T19, B, D16
	T19, T14, D20
140	T20, T20, D10
	T18, T18, D16
	T20, D20, D20

Details

131

T20, T13, D16 – T20, T17, D10 – T17, D20, D20

Most players start this combination with T20. If you hit it, then depending on your preference, you can either go for T13 or T17 with the second dart.

If you hit single 20 with the first dart, you are left with 111, which is another dart at T20. If it goes in, you are left with 51, which is an easy setup for the next turn.

How To Master The Art Of Finishing

If you hit two single 20's with the first two darts, you are left with 91, which is T17 with your last dart to leave D20 (or 74 if you hit single 17).

If your opponent is on a good finish, and you are in a do or die situation, then you might want to look at going for T17, D20, and D20. The doubles are a bigger target than the trebles, so why not go all out for it? If you miss, at least you went out on your sword, trying to the very end. And if it goes in, then everything changes. It hurts your opponent more than anything (other than winning the match), and it gives you a massive boost of confidence and adrenalin. These are the types of shots that turn matches around, and are so unforgettable that you will still be talking about it years later!

Of course, out-shots presented here are not the only ways this finish can be taken out. You can just as easily start with T19, which if successful leaves 74. Or even T15, which leaves 86. The point I will make though, is that knowing all these just for the sake of knowing them is not the purpose of this book. The purpose is to know the ones that offer the best percentage chances of success, and to go for the ones that make the most sense, given the situation you are in at any given moment in a match.

In other words, keep it as simple as possible, and use the dartboard to your advantage. You throw at the T20, T19 and T18 more than any other trebles, so use them in finishing combinations whenever possible – as long as it makes good sense to do so. That way you are keeping the odds of success on your side as much as is feasibly possible. Finishing is hard enough to begin with. Don't make it any harder for yourself than you have to.

132
B, B, D16 – B, T14, D20 – O/B, T19, B

On the face of it, this may look like an extravagant way to go for this finish. For sure, it is one of THE most glamorous out-shots you can get, and hitting B, B, D16 is about as difficult as it gets. But there are very valid reasons as to why this is the way to go for this finish.

If you start the shot on the 20's or 19's, and only hit the single, then that's it; you cannot finish this turn. Single 20 leaves a remaining balance of 112 and a single 19 leaves a total of 113. Neither of which can be achieved in two darts. So, rule this out straight away when your opponent is on a finish.

By going for the bullseye with the first dart, you give yourself a margin of error. If your first dart lands in the O/B, you can still finish the shot. You are left with 107, which is T19, B. Not easy for sure, but you still have a chance.

If the first dart lands in the bullseye and is a great marker for the second; go right back at it. If you hit it, then you are on for one of the best out-shots on the entire dartboard.

If you hit the bullseye with the first dart and you block it for a second dart, then throw at the T14 for D20. Single 14 will leave 60. This will leave an easy set up for the next time at the oche.

Another good reason for going for it in this manner is that if your first dart lands in the bullseye, and is inviting a second dart to nestle right in there alongside it, is that if you hit the O/B, you will require 57, which is a simple single 17 to leave D20 – and hope you get a chance to get a go at it next turn.

If your opponent is not on a finish, then you don't need to go for it this way. You can set it up for the next turn. For instance, you can throw for a straight ton to leave D16 when you return.

133

T20, T19, D8 – T19, D19, D19

T20, T19, D8 is the recognized method of going for this finish. There is no room for error, and the odds of hitting it are low, even for advanced players. But that doesn't mean that you don't go for it in the correct manner. And when it does go in, it is euphoric!!

Another method sometimes used by the top players is to go for T19, D19, and D19. This is only to be used when you are in a dire situation, and you simply have to get it this turn or risk losing the game. It is one of those high risk/high reward shots that are a revelation when they pay off.

If you hit single 20 with the first dart, you are left with 113, which can be T20 again. This leaves 53 which is a simple setup shot for next time (and hope that you get another chance at getting it).

If the T20 is blocked by the first dart, or if you just prefer going for the 19's in this situation, then T19 leaves 56, which again is an easy setup for the next turn.

If your first two darts are in single 20, you are left with 93, which is T19 for D18, and if your first two darts are in the single 20 and single 19, you then require 94, which is a dart at the T18 for D20.

If you decided to go the T19, D19, D19 route, and hit single 19 with the first dart, there is nothing wrong with going right back for the T19 again with the second dart. If you hit it, you are left on 57, which is single 17 to leave D20 next time (if there is a next time).

Of course, this isn't the only way to take this shot out. There are plenty of other options open to you. You could, for instance, go for T17 with the first dart. This leaves you on 82. Single 17 leaves 116, that will leave T19, single 19 to leave 40, or T20, 20 to leave D18, or T20, single 16 to leave 40.

It's good to be aware of other options, but keep to the ones that give you the best possible chance of success. In this case, it is T20, T19, D8.

134
T20, T14, D16 – T20, T18, D10 – T18, D20, D20

This is another one of those finishes that can be taken out with a treble/double/double combination. This is only to be used when you have your back to the wall and are in a do or die situation, otherwise go for it in the more conventional manner.

The first dart should be at T20. If you hit it, then you have options on the 74 that is remaining.

If your first dart goes into single 20, you will be left with 114. This is T20 again, which leaves 54.

If your first dart is in single 20 and blocks the treble, then you can go for T18 with the second dart. If you hit it, you will be left with 60, which is a simple setup to leave D20 next time.

135
B, T15, D20 – B, T19, D14 – O/B, T20, B – T19, T18, D12

This is another of the unique out-shots that is best served by throwing for the bullseye first. It gives you some room for error in that you can hit either the bullseye or the O/B with the first dart and still be able to complete the finish. When the dartboard offers you opportunities like this, take them.

If you hit the bullseye, you are left with 85. If you hit the O/B, you are left with 110, which is a two-dart finish, T20, B.

If the second dart lands in the single 20, you are left with 90. With one dart remaining, you can throw for T18 to leave D18, or the bullseye again to leave D20.

Of course, if your opponent is not on a finish, you can go for this shot in any way you choose. For instance, T20 leaves 75, which is T17, D12. If you go for the T19 with the first dart, you would be left with 78, which is T18, D12.

A good benefit from going the T19 route is that 95 leaves D20, so if you are under no pressure to finish on this turn, you can leave a great double and not have to move away from the same number.

136
T20, T20, D8 – T16, T16, D20

There is really only one way to go for this, and that is T20, T20, and D8. Even if you don't hit it (and the vast majority of times you won't), you can put pressure on your opponent by hitting 20, T20, 16 to leave D20 next turn.

Remember, if you cannot take the finish out on that particular turn, your job is then to put as much pressure as you possibly can on your opponent by leaving a good finish for the next turn.

Of course, there are other ways of getting 136. You could go for T16, T16, D20, or T18, B, D16. As always though, keep to the percentages. You throw at the T20 more than anything else on the dartboard, so use that in your finishing selections whenever it makes sense to do so. With this finish, always go for it with T20, T20, and D8.

The only exception to going for T20, T20, and D8 is if your first dart is in the T20 and is either blocking another dart from joining it, or is hanging precariously and throwing another dart at it would probably knock it out. In this scenario, assuming your opponent is on a good finish, it might be a good idea to go the double/double route. You would be on 72, so D20, D16 or D18, D18 would be good choices. Again, only use this method if you are in a dire situation and you either get the finish or risk losing the game. Otherwise, stick to the more traditional methods.

137
T20, T19, D10 – T19, T16, D16 – T19, D20, D20

There is no advantage to be gained by going for either treble with the first dart, so starting on either is fine. Most players seem to go for T20 with the first dart, and this makes sense because it is the area of the board you throw at the most often.

If you do throw for T20 first, and hit the single, you will be on 117, which is T20 again to leave 57 with one dart remaining. If you hit single 20 with your second dart, then you will be on 97, which is T19, to leave D20 when (and if) you return to the oche.

If your first dart is in single 20, you could throw for T19 with the second. If you hit it, you would be left with 60, which is a simple setup shot for the next turn.

If you went for T19 with the first dart and hit the single, you would be left with 118. The second dart should then be thrown at the T20 to leave 58 after two darts.

You could throw again for the T19, but this leaves 61, which is above 60 (remember, you want to get to 60 or below whenever possible so you can set up a good double with the last dart). 61 is a decent enough setup shot if you hit the O/B to leave D18, but going T20 with the second dart is probably the better way to go with this combination.

Another good option for when your opponent is on a good finish, is to go for T19, D20, D20. This is yet another of the high risk/high reward shots that are worth taking on when you are in dire trouble and simply have to get it.

138
T20, T18, D12 – T19, T19, D12 – T20, T20, D9

This is the shot made famous by Keith Deller in the 1983 Embassy World Professional Darts Championship final. Needing just one more leg to win the title, unseeded qualifier Deller was left on 138.

How To Master The Art Of Finishing

World number one and heavy favorite Eric Bristow was throwing first, and needed 121. He hit single 17, and then T18. He needed the bullseye to level the match in the final set. Instead, he threw his last dart into the single 18, setting up D16 on his next turn. That was his fatal mistake. Keith Deller walked up to the oche, and planted T20, T18, D12 to win the world title. The moral of this story is to never assume that your opponent will miss his finish. Always assume the worst, and if you are able to have a go at a finish, then do so.

Traditionally, T20, T18, D12 has been the way to go for this out-shot. However, in recent times, going for T19, T19, and D12 has become more popular. This is because you don't have to switch if you hit the first T19, just stay there and go right back at it. It makes sense go this way.

If you are up against it, and prefer the T20, then going for it again and then throwing for D9 is also an option. When you only have one dart at a double or risk losing the game, it really doesn't matter which double it is; they are all the same size.

If you go the 19 route and hit the single, then you are left with 119. In this case, stay on the 19's with the second dart. If you hit the single 19 again you are on 100, which is T20 with the last dart. If you hit T19 with the second dart, you are on 62, which is either T10 or T14, depending on what double you want to leave.

If you go the 20 route and hit the single with the first dart, you are left with 118. Stay on the 20 with the second dart. If you hit the treble you will leave 58, which is an easy set up for the next time. If you hit another single, you are left with 98. This is T20 again, leaving a less than ideal 38 when (and if) you return. This is one more reason the 19 route is probably the better choice with this shot.

139
T20, T13, D20 – T20, T19, D11 – T19, B, D16 – T19, T14, D20

Most players start this combination on the T20. If you hit it, you are left with 79, which leaves a couple of options as can be seen in the charts.

The T19 route is also a viable option, and there is nothing wrong in going for it this way.

If you go the T20 route and hit the single with the first dart, you are on 119. You could stay there again, and if you hit the T20 you will be on 59, which is an easy setup for next time. If both your first two darts are in the single 20, you will be on 99, which is T19 with the last dart to try to leave 42 for next time.

If the first dart is in the single 20, you could throw for the 19 with the second dart. If you hit the treble, you are on 62, which is either T10 or T14 with the last dart, depending on your preferred double. If your second dart hits the single 19, you are on 100, which is a dart at T20 for D20.

If you go the 19 route and hit the single with the first dart, you are then on 120. This is T20, 20 to leave 40 on the next turn.

140
T20, T20, D10 – T18, T18, D16 - T20, D20, D20

The vast majority of players go for this finish using the T20 option. If you hit the treble with the first dart and then block it for a second dart, or if your back is against the wall and you simply have to get it, throw for the double/double combination to create mayhem and win the leg in style!!

2018 World Champion Rob Cross famously took out 140 this way to win the World Title against the retiring Phil Taylor. Pro player Dave Chisnall also goes for it this way, but not many others do. It does leave a good double in D16, but there is no advantage to be gained by going this way. The T20 route also leaves a good double (D10), and is the recommended way to go for this finish.

The 20 route gives you the best percentage shot at this. Not only for the fact that 20 is thrown at more than any other segment on the board, but also if you hit a single instead of the treble. If you hit T20 and single 20 - in any order – then you will be on 60, which is another 20 to leave D20 next time around.

In other words, a straight ton leaves you on D20, which is the best you can hope to do if you cannot take it out on this particular turn.

If you take the 18 options and hit the single and treble, you would be left with 68. This is above our target of 60 or below, and requires another treble to set up three clear darts at a double on the next turn.

Chapter 9 Quiz

1. How would you go for 131? What if your opponent was sitting on D16 for the match? What would you do then? Why?
2. Why is starting on the bullseye the best way to go for a 132 out-shot? What would you do if your first dart was in the O/B and your opponent was on a good finish? Why?
3. What is the best way to go for 133? Why? What is an alternative that is high risk/high reward?
4. You are on 134, and your opponent is sitting on 32 for the match. What are your options with this out-shot? What are you going to do? Why?
5. You are on 135. What is the best way of going for this out-shot? Why? What would you do differently if your opponent is not on a finish? Why?
6. You are on 136. How are you going to go for this finish? What would you do if your opponent was on D20 and your first dart was in the T20 but blocking a second dart from joining it? Why? What would you do in this same situation except that your opponent was not on a finish? Why?
7. You are on 137, and your opponent is on 62. What are your choices with this finish? How are you going to go for it? Why?
8. You are on 138. Regardless of where your opponent is sitting, how are you going to go for this out-shot? Why?
9. You are on 139. What are your options with this out-shot? How are you going to go for it? Why?
10. You are on 140. What are your options with this out-shot? With your opponent on a good finish, what would you do if your first dart was in the T20 but blocking another from joining it? Why?

Chapter Ten: 141-150

The finishes just keep getting harder and harder, and it's important to know that even the professionals don't get these finishes very often, and when they do they usually show their delight with a fist pump and a look of self-satisfaction etched on their faces.

The further up the competitive ladder you get, the more you will see shots like these taken out, and you need to be ready for it when it happens to you. It can be very demoralizing when you have played very well, and are sitting on a double to take the game, only to stand there and watch your opponent take out a huge three figure finish.

What is vital with these out-shots is to know what to go for when you are not able to finish on that particular turn. It is essential to choose the correct shot selection to set yourself up for a good finish on the next turn, assuming you get one. If you have studied the previous chapters diligently, you will know instinctively what to go for when you find yourself in this situation, which you will be most of the time.

Number	Solution
141	T20, T19, D12 T20, T15, D18 T17, T18, D18
142	T20, B, D16 T20, T14, D20 T20, T20, D11 T17, T17, D20

143	T20, T17, D16
	T19, T18, D16
144	T20, T20, D12
	T18, T18, D18
145	T20, T15, D20
	T20, T19, D14
146	T20, T18, D16
	T19, T19, D16
	T20, T20, D13
147	T20, T17, D18
	T19, T18, D18
	T19, B, D20
148	T20, T20, D14
	T18, T18, D20
	T20, T16, D20
149	T20, T19, D20
150	T20, T18, D18
	T19, T19, D18
	T20, T20, D15
	T20, B, D20
	B, B, B

Details

141

T20, T19, D12 – T20, T15, D18 – T17, T18, D18

This is the finish that is typically taken out for a perfect 9 dart game of 501. You see this quite regularly at the very top level nowadays, because the standards of the top players have gone through the roof.

Phil Taylor hit two perfect games in one match, during the 2010 Premier League final against James Wade, and even came very close to a third!! Michael van Gerwen missed D12 for back to back 9 dart legs in the semi-finals of the World Championships in 2013, also against James Wade.

James Wade then found himself creating another piece of history in the 2014 World Grand Prix in Ireland when both he and Robert Thornton hit the perfect 9 dart game during the same match, except this time it was with a double start!!

The great John Lowe hit the first ever televised 9 dart leg back in 1984, in the MFI World Matchplay. He finished with T17, T18, and D18 after hitting 2X180 with his first two visits to the board. He collected £100,000 for his efforts, which equates to over £11,000 per dart!

Paul Lim is still the only player to hit the perfect game in the Lakeside World Championships – more commonly known as the BDO World Championships. He completed his feat in 1990, and it made him more famous at the time than the eventual winner of the tournament!! The winner that year was an unknown and unseeded player called Phil Taylor. He has since gone on to win 16 World titles, before retiring as a losing finalist at the 2018 World Championships. He is widely considered to be the greatest darts player of all time.

Paul Lim wired D12 for the 9-darter against Gary Anderson in round 2 of the 2018 World Championships. If he had managed to get it, he would have become the only player to hit perfect games in both versions of the World Championships, and - incredibly – he would have managed it 28 years apart!!

I know I digressed, and not all 9 dart legs are finished on 141, but no matter how many perfect games are hit due to the incredible standards the players have reached these days, I never tire of watching them, or seeing the reactions of both the players and the fans watching in disbelief as the final double goes in to complete the perfect game. I'm sure you feel the same too.

Back to the finishes:

The recognized method of getting 141 is T20, T19, D12, although going for T20, T15, and D18 is also a popular method. Either way works well; it comes down to personal preference as to which double you want to leave at the end of the combination.

If you hit single 20 with the first dart, you are on 121. You have a plethora of options with this, but assuming you have not blocked the T20, you can go right back for it. If you get it, you will be on 61, which is O/B to leave D18, or T15 to leave D8. If your second dart also goes in single 20, you will be on 101. You can go for the T20 again to leave 41, or T19 to leave 44.

The bullseye plays a more integral role with the finishes in this chapter, and here's why:

As mentioned above, it is as much about what you leave yourself with these out-shots as it is about taking them out with 3 darts.

In the previous chapters, you discovered that leaving yourself below 61 with the last dart is what you strive for if you can't take it out on that particular turn. This is one of the six major numbers all 501 players should be aware of. Another is 81, and it is this number that we are concentrating on in this chapter.

How To Master The Art Of Finishing

All six of the major numbers are covered in depth in my book *The Seven Pillars of Darts*, which you can obtain for free at *www.DartsFinishing.com/Pillars*.

Let's say that you hit single 20 with the first 2 darts. You are now left on 101 with one dart left. You could go back for a big treble with the last dart, and there is nothing wrong with that.

But think about it for a second. If you hit another 20 you would be on 81. Unless you hit a treble, this is a 3-dart finish on the bullseye – which is a lot more difficult than leaving yourself on a double.

Instead, throw the last dart at the bullseye. In this instance you would be left with 51 if you hit it, which is a good 2-dart out on a double.

If you hit the O/B – and this is why this shot is recommended – you will be left with 76, and *this can be finished on a double rather than the bullseye*.

There may only be five points in it, but those five points make a world of difference to your odds of getting the finish – and that is what this method is all about.

The other option with 81 (first 2 darts in single 20) is to go for T19 with the last dart. Treble would leave you on 44, and the single 82. 82 is a decent 3 dart out-shot because you can use the bullseye with the first dart. As always, learn the options and choose your favored method.

Advanced strategic knowledge such as this puts you head and shoulders above the vast majority of your opponents, and is the difference between winning and losing.

If you went the 17 route and hit single 17 with the first dart, you are left with 124. Throw the second dart at T20. If you hit it, you are on 64, which is T16/T8 with the last dart.

If you hit single 20 with the second dart, you are left with 104. You can then throw the last dart at T20 to try to leave 44, or T18 to leave 50.

Or you could use the strategy explained above and throw it at the bullseye. If you hit it, you are left with 54, which gives you two darts at a double next turn. The O/B leaves you on 79 - which brings you below 81.

This strategy should guarantee you at least one dart at a double on the next turn. If you had thrown for the 20 again and hit the single, you would be left on 84. Unless you hit a treble, you would only get one dart at the bullseye for the win.

142
T20, B, D16 – T20, T14, D20 – T20, T20, D11 – T17, T17, D20

There are a few ways of going for this finish, and if you start on the T20, it really depends on what your opponent has left as to how you approach it.

If your opponent is on a good finish, then shot selection becomes critical, and you have to squeeze every advantage you possibly can out of the dartboard. If your first dart is in the T20 and is a good marker for a second; go right back at it to try to leave D11. At the end of the day, if you only have one dart at a double then it doesn't matter which double it is. You either hit it or you don't. Going for it with this method gives you a better percentage chance over going the traditional way of T20, B, D16 because you are not switching all over the board with each of the three darts.

If you hit single 20 with the first dart, you are left with 122. With just two darts left in your hands, stay on the 20 with the second dart (unless the treble is blocked. In that case move to the T18 with the second dart, or even the bullseye). If the second dart hits the T20, you

How To Master The Art Of Finishing

will require 62. The third dart can then be at either T10 or T14, depending on your double preference.

If the second dart lands in single 20, you are left with 102. This is where the advanced strategy comes into play. You can throw for T20 again, trying to leave 42. If it lands in the single, you will be on 82 when you return. You could also throw the last dart at the bullseye. If you hit it you will require 52, and the O/B leaves you on 77.

In this particular instance there is no real advantage to be gained by going for the bullseye with the last dart. If you require 82, you throw at the bullseye with the first dart on the next turn. Even the O/B leaves 57, which should give you one dart at D20. If you require 77 and hit the single 19 with the first dart on the next turn, you will still only get one dart at a double. So, in this situation, you are probably better off trying to hit a large treble to bring your score down as far as you can with the last dart.

More and more, players are using grouping to stack the odds more in their favor. With 142, the T17 opens up this opportunity for you. If you hit T17 with the first dart, go right back at it. If the second dart follows it into the treble, you are left with D20 for a great finish.

If your first dart hits single 17, you are left with 125. Your second dart could then be thrown at the bullseye. If you hit it, you will require 75, which is right back at T17 again for D12. You could even throw at the bullseye again to leave either 25 or 50 when you return.

If the second dart goes in the O/B, you will require 100 with one dart left. That is T20 for D20.

If you hit the T17 with the first dart, you are then on 91. At this stage, because you have studied the earlier chapters diligently, you know instinctively what to go for no matter where the second dart lands. This way it takes all the mathematics out of the equation and prevents big pauses in your game while you work out what to do next. These pauses take you out of your rhythm and can cause you to mess up the shot.

This is why it is imperative that you always know what number you are left with at all times. T17, D20 is 91. Do it enough times and there is no thinking required, no mathematics required, nothing. It is an automatic response to what you instinctively already know. And this is how you master the art of finishing.

In this scenario, you have hit the T17 and single 17 with the first two darts. Without missing a beat, you instinctively know that you require 74 with one dart remaining. Without any mathematics whatsoever, and with absolute fluency, your last dart is aimed at either T14 or T18, depending on your double preference.

143
T20, T17, D16 – T19, T18, D16

Just about every player goes for this with the T20 method. I only included the T19 method for clarity, and to show that there are always options.

If your first dart hit T20, you are left with 83. You know instinctively that this is T17 with the second dart.

If the first dart lands in single 20, you are on 123. This could be either T20 or T19. T20 leaves 63, which is T13 with the last dart. T19 leaves 66, which has several options with the last dart.

If you hit the T20 with the first dart, and then the single 17 with the second, you are again left with 66. Hopefully by now you have seen the patterns the dartboard keeps giving to you?

If the first dart is in single 20, and the second dart goes in single 19, you are left with 104. The last dart could be thrown at either T20 or T18.

However, if you use the advanced strategy with the last dart, you will realize that single 20 or 19 leaves you above the important pillar number of 81. 20 will leave 83, and 19 leaves 84.

If you went for the bullseye instead, you would get yourself under 81, and therefore greatly increase your odds of finishing it on the next turn.

If the first 2 darts were single 20 and single 19, then the bullseye would leave you on 54, which is a great 2 dart out-shot, and O/B would leave 79. Although this potentially leaves an odd double (11), it also allows you to set up a good double (D20) if the first dart doesn't hit T19.

I know I keep beating on about percentages, but this is so important that I make no apologies for it. It really does make THAT much difference.

144

T20, T20, D12 – T18, T18, D18

This is another finish that is found at the end of the fabled 9 dart leg. In fact, it is probably thrown for just as much as the 141, because it is seen to be slightly more gettable due to the fact that both the first two darts are at the same target and there is no switching around the board to leave a double.

To do this, the player has to get a 180 and a 177 to leave the 144 finish. For most players, this is an impossible dream, but it is a dream that all players strive for.

The vast majority of players use the T20 method with this shot, and it makes perfect sense to do so. You throw at the T20 more than at any other segment of the board, so use it whenever you can as part of your finishing strategy.

Of course, there are always other options, and they are useful to know. If your first dart lands in the T20, and then either blocks another one from following it, or it is hanging precariously, it is better to try a different route with the second dart.

Without skipping a beat, you instinctively know that you have 84 left. You also know that T16 leaves D18, so your second dart is straight at the that target. If you hit the single 16, you are left with 68. Normally this would be T20 for D4, but in this scenario the T20 is blocked and we can't use it.

That's okay though, because you know that another T16 leaves D10, so that is what you aim at with the third dart. You also have the option of T12 to leave D16, so even if the second dart blocked the T16 you still have a good option to leave a double when you return.

If the first dart lands in the single 20, you require 124. Throw your second dart right back at the T20. If it hits, you are on 64, which is T16/T8. If it lands in the single, you are on 104. This can be again at the T20, or T18, or even the bullseye.

Single 20 with the second dart leaves you on 104. Single again leaves 84 when you return. If you throw the last dart at the bullseye, you will be left with either 54 or 79, which gives you at least one dart at a double when you return.

Hopefully by now you have realized that all these finishes keep ending up leaving pretty much the same numbers when you break them down. Once learned, this is a huge advantage to the player that has taken the time to learn them, and it gives you a massive edge.

If you decide to go the 18 route, T18 leaves 90. If the treble is then blocked, you have the option of going for the bullseye to leave D20, or even T20 to leave D15 (if your opponent is on a good finish).

Single 18 with the first dart will leave 126. With two darts, this is T20 to leave 66, or even T19 to leave 69.

If the first dart is in single 18, and the second lands in single 20, you are left with 106. The advanced strategy only works when you are on 105 or below after 2 darts, so in this instance it is not advisable to throw for the bullseye as there is no strategic advantage from doing so.

Instead, throw at a big treble to try to bring your score down as much as possible. T20 would leave 45, and T19 would leave 48.

Because the T20 route allows the advanced strategy to come into play, and because it allows you to bring your score below 81 without hitting a treble, this is the recommended method of going for this shot.

145

T20, T15, D20 – T20, T19, D14

Just about every player starts this combination on T20. If you get it, then you have the option of either T15 or T19, depending on your preferences.

If your first dart goes into T20, and the second dart hits the single 15, you are left on 70, which is either T18 or T10 with the last dart.

If your first dart is in the T20 and the second goes into single 19, you are left on 66 (this number comes up a lot if you follow the patterns). You then have several options to setup your finish for the next turn.

If your first dart goes into the single 20, you will be left on 125. You could throw for the bullseye with the second dart, but it is more advisable to stay on the T20 (unless it is blocked by the first dart). If you hit it, you will be on 65, which is a good setup for the next turn with the O/B to leave D20.

If your second dart also lands in the single 20, you will be left with 105. If you hit the T20 with the last dart, you will be left with 45 when you return. Another single 20 leaves you with 85 when you return, which could only give you one dart at the bullseye to take the finish.

The advanced option would be to go for the bullseye with the final dart. If you hit it, you will be left with 55, which is a good two dart finish when you return. If you hit the O/B, you would be left with 80, which means that you can assure yourself of at least one dart at D20 on your next turn.

Going for it in this manner gives you slightly better odds than if you had left 85, because it gives you a dart at a double rather than the bullseye. As always, it comes down to personal preference, but it the board offers you any advantages, it is wise to at least know them and have them in your armory for when you need them.

Naturally, there are other ways of getting this finish. For instance, you could go for T19 with the first dart. If you get it you are left with 88, which is either T20 or T16, depending on your preferred double.

You could even start the shot on the bullseye if you wanted to impress your friends and anyone else that was watching at the time. Bullseye would leave you 95, which is T19, D19. Or you could go even more dramatic and go for T15, B. That would be a real barnstormer of a finish!!

Most of the time you will not have the luxury of going for exotic out-shots like the one described above. Usually, you will be involved in a tight game where your shot selection is critical to the outcome of the match. So T20 is the way to go with this finish.

146
T20, T18, D16 – T19, T19, D16 – T20, T20, D13

More and more, players are starting to use the T19 for this finish, and it's easy to see why. Rather than switch from the T20 to the T18, you can stay right where you are on the T19, and go right back at it with the second dart. It makes good sense.

If your first dart goes in the T19, you will be left with 89. If the second dart then lands in the single 19, you will know instinctively that you are left with 70, which can be either T18 or T10, depending on your double preference.

If your first dart is in single 19, you will be left with 127. You can stay on T19 with the second dart, or go up to the T20 if you prefer. T19 would leave you on 70 (as explained in the above paragraph), and T20 leaves you on 67, which is T17 for D8 (T9 for D20 if you are so inclined).

If both the first two darts go in the single 19, you would be left with 108, which is T19 again to leave 51 when you return. Another single 19 leaves 89 when you return.

Going for the bullseye is not an option once you get past 145, because if you hit the O/B with 146 or higher you cannot get below the threshold of 81. Remember, the advanced strategy only works when you are left on 105 or lower after 2 darts.

If you hit the single 20 with the first dart, you would be left with 126. If the T20 bed is still unblocked after the first dart, you could go right back at it to leave 66 (that number again) with one dart remaining. Another single 20 leaves 106, which is again at the T20 to leave 46 when you return.

If the first dart is in the single 20, and you throw at T19 with the second dart, you would be left with 69 if you hit it. This could then be either T19 again to leave D6, or T15 to leave D12. If you hit single 19 with the second dart, you would be left with 107, which is T19 again to leave 50 when you return. Another single leaves 88.

147
T20, T17, D18 – T19, T18, D18 – T19, B, D20

Most players go the T20 route with this finish, although the T19 method is viable as well.

T20 and then single 17 leaves 70, which is T18 or T10 to leave your favored double. Single 20 will leave 127, which is either T20 or T19 with the second dart.

If the T20 is open, go right back at it. If you get it, you are left on 67, which is T17 for D8. Another single 20 leaves 107, which is T19 to leave 50, or T20 again to leave 47.

If you went for T19 with the second dart, after hitting the single 20 with the first, you would be on 70 if you hit it (do you see the pattern with this finish?)

If your second dart landed in the single 19, you would be left with 108, which is T19 again to leave 51 when you return. You could also go back for the T20, which would leave 48, or single leaves 88.

When throwing for the combination shots, if the first dart land in the single but gives you a good marker for the second dart to go for the treble, then stay there and go for it. In this particular instance it makes no difference if you leave 67 or 70 after the second dart. Both require a treble to leave a double, and both are good out-shots. Take the percentage shot whenever you can. It will dramatically increase your chances of success.

148
T20, T20, D14 – T18, T18, D20 – T20, T16, D20

Most players go for this with T20, T20, D14. The reason is simple: It utilizes the percentages more than any other method available.

If you hit the T20 with the first dart, then go right back at it (assuming the first dart didn't block the treble). If it goes in, you are then on D14.

If it lands in the single 20, you are on 68, which is right back at the T20 again to leave D4. As long as you stay straight in the 20 bed, you don't have to move away from it with any of the three darts. Even a straight ton leaves 48, which is a good two-dart out on the next visit.

If the treble 20 is blocked, or if you have the luxury of time, then T16 with the second dart is an option to leave D20. It makes a lot more sense, however, to stay on the 20's if at all possible. The odds are much better for you if you do.

Dave Chisnall is a professional player that sometimes goes the T18 route with this finish. It's easy to see why, as 2x T18 leaves D20. If you hit the treble with the first dart, and then single with the second, you will be left with 76, which is T20 for D8. Single 20 will leave 56 when you return on the next visit.

If your first dart lands in the single 18, you will require 130. The second dart should be at T20, which leaves 70 with the last dart. A single 20 leaves you on 110, which is T20 again to leave 50. Single 20 again leaves 90 when you return on the next visit.

Because you throw at the 20 more than any other segment of the board, and because you don't have to switch away from the 20 at all with this shot (unless the first two darts are in the treble of course), it is highly recommended that you use this route on this finish.

149

T20, T19, D16

There is only one way to sensibly go for this, and that is T20, T19, and D16. If the first dart is in T20, and the second in single 19, you are left with 70 with the last dart, which is either T10 or T18, depending on your preference.

If the first dart is in single 20, you are on 129. You have options here. You can go back at the T20 to leave 69, or T19 to leave 72.

If both of the first two darts are in the single 20, you are left with 109. Again, you have the choice of either the T20 or T19 with the third dart. T20 leaves 49, and T19 leaves 52, both good two darts outs when you return on the next visit.

If your first two darts are single 20 and single 19, you are left with 110. This is T20 again to leave 50 when you return. You could even go back at the T19 with the last dart to leave 53. Both are two dart out-shots when you return on the next visit, so there is no advantage either way.

If all three darts are in the single bed, scoring 59, then you are left with 90 when you return on the next visit. How you approach this when you return depends on what your opponent has left, as detailed earlier in the book.

150

T20, T18, D18 – T19, T19, D18 – T20, T20, D15 – T20, B, D20

B, B, B

There are several viable options with this finish, but more and more players are going for it with T19. This makes sense because you have two darts at the same treble before throwing for the double. The same can be said by going for the T20 first, but the T19 route leaves a better double.

If you do decide to go the T19 route and hit T19, 19 with the first two darts, you are left with 74, which is either T18 or T14 with the last dart.

If your first dart is in single 19 you are on 131. You can stay right where you are on the 19's, or go back up top for the T20. T19 leaves 74 as we have already discovered, and T20 leaves 71, which is either T13 or T17 with the last dart.

If both the first two darts are in single 19, you are left with 112, which is T20 to leave 52, or single 20 leaves 92 when you return.

If the first two darts are in single 19 and single 20, you are on 111, which will leave plenty of options. T20 leaves 51 (single leaves 91). T19 leaves 54 (single leaves 92), and T17 leaves 60 (single leaves 94). Choose your option and go for it.

If you go the T20 route and hit T20/20 with the first two darts, scoring 80 points, you are left on 70 with the last dart. If both darts are in single 20, you are on 110, which is T20 again to leave 50. Score 60 with all three darts, and you are left with 90 when you return.

If you decide to go the T20/T18 route, and the first two darts are in T20, single 18, you are left with 72 with one dart remaining.

Chapter 10 Quiz

1. You require 141. Your first dart goes in the T20, and the second lands in the single 19. What number are you left on? What are your options? How are you going to go for it? Why?
2. You require 142. What options do you have with this finish? How are you going to approach it? Why?
3. You require 143. Your first dart is in single 20. What are your options with the last two darts? How are you going to throw for it? Why?
4. You require 144. Your first dart is in the T20 and is blocking the second dart from joining it. What are your options in this situation? What are you going to do? Why?
5. You require 145. Your first dart lands in T20. What are your options with the second dart? How are you going to go for it? Why? What will you do if you hit the single with the second dart? Why?
6. You require 146. You have some good options with this finish. You decide to go the T19 route. The first dart lands in T19, and the second goes in the single 19. What do you have left? What are you going to do with the last dart? Why?
7. You require 147. What are your options with this finish? How are you going to go for it? Why?
8. You require 148. What are your options with this finish? How are you going to go for it? Why?
9. You require 149. What are your options with this out-shot? How are you going to go for it? Why?
10. You require 150. You have several good options with this out-shot. How are you going to approach the finish? Why?

Chapter Eleven: 151-160

Not all the finishes in this chapter are three dart finishes. Unless you have no alternative, never leave yourself on 159 as there is no way to take this out in three darts. All you are doing is handing your opponent an extra opportunity or three extra darts by leaving this number.

You are now in the realm of the super finishes, the ones that grabs everybody's attention. However, when you break it down, they are no more difficult that any of the others from 131 and above. They may be higher numbers, but they are still the same finish – two trebles and a double combination. If you can take out 131, you can take out 160.

Of course, these are highly advanced finishes, and you are not going to take them out very often. That is why it is so important to know what you have left after every dart, and to make the correct shot each and every time. Hopefully, by now, you will have that down and ingrained in your brain.

Number	Solution
151	T20, T17, D20 T19, T18, D20
152	T20, T20, D16
153	T20, T19, D18
154	T20, T18, D20 T19, T19, D20

155	T20, T19, D19
156	T20, T20, D18
157	T20, T19, D20
158	T20, T20, D19
159	No Finish
160	T20, T20, D20

Details

151
T20, T17, D20 – T19, T18, D20

Almost every player goes for this shot on the treble 20. If you hit it, you are left with 91, which as can be seen is T17, D20. If the second dart goes in the single 17, you are on 74 with the last dart.

If the first dart goes in the single 20, you are on 131. T20 would be a good shot again with the second dart. If you hit it, you are on 71 with the last dart.

If it goes in the single 20 again, you are left with 111. Again, T20 would be a good target to aim at. If you hit it, you are on 51, which is a good two-dart out when you return.

If all three-darts land in the single 20, you are left with 91 when you return.

As in the previous chapter, you could always use the advanced bullseye technique with the last dart. 91 is another of the pillar numbers that you need to get below if at all possible.

If the first 2 darts are both in single 20, you have the option to throw the last dart at the bullseye. If it goes in, you will be on 61 when you return. If it goes in the O/B, you will have 86 when you return, which is a better finish to leave than 91.

If you recall from previous chapters, 91 requires you to hit a treble to leave a double. If your opponent is on a finish, then you may be forced to go the bullseye route with the first dart. Hit it and you have a good shot at taking it out. If you hit the O/B, you then have to throw for 16, B or T16, D9.

If instead you leave yourself on 86, you have potentially better odds of taking it out. T18 leaves D16, 18, T18 leaves D7, or two single 18's leaves the bullseye.

You don't have to go this way, but it is a good option if you choose to take it.

152

T20, T20, D16

There is only one way to go for this (unless you are showing off and want to go T20, T14, B, which is obviously not recommended!).

If the first two darts score 80 points, you are left with 72 with the last dart. You could stay on the T20 to leave 12, or go for either T16 or T12, depending on your preferences.

If the first two darts score 40 points, you are on 112. This is again at T20 with the last dart to leave 52, or 92 if you hit another single 20.

If both the first 2 darts are in single 20, you have the option to throw the last one at the bullseye. If you hit it, you will be left with 62 when you return. If you hit the O/B, you will require 87 when you return, which is a better finish than 92.

153
T20, T19, D18

The higher the finishes are the less available options you have to get them. In this instance, there is no other way to get this finish.

If you hit 79 with the first two darts, you are on 74 with the last dart. If the first dart is in single 20, you are left with 133. Go for the T20 again to bring the score down as much as you possibly can with the second dart. If it goes in, you are left with 73 with the last dart. Go for the T19, and if you hit it and score 137, you have left yourself on D8. That is a good shot to make.

If you score 40 with the first two darts, you are on 113. Again, throw at the treble 20 (or 19 of course) with the last dart. If it goes in, you are left with 53 when you return. Another single leaves you with 93 when you return.

As above, you also have the option of throwing the last dart at the bullseye. Hit it and you leave yourself 63 when you return. If you hit the O/B, you will leave yourself on 88 when you return, which is a better finish than 93.

154
T20, T18, D20 – T19, T19, D20

Although most players go for this shot with the T20, more and more are seeing the benefits of going the T19 route. You have two darts at the same treble as opposed to switching around the board.

If you do go the T20 route and score 78 with the first two darts, you are left on 76 with the last dart, which is right back at the T20 to leave D8.

If the first dart is in the single 20, go right back at it again and score as much as you can with the second dart. Score 80 with the first two darts and you are left on 74 with one dart remaining. Score 60 with all three darts and you require 94 when you return.

If you go the T19 route, and score 76 with the first two darts, you are on 78 with the last dart, which is T18 to leave D12 when you return. Score 38 with the first two darts, and you are on 116. You could go up to the T20 to leave 56, or stay on the T19 to leave 59. Either is a good choice.

Score 57 with three darts, and you are on 97 when you return. Score 58 with three darts and you leave 96 when you return.

The advanced bullseye technique only works if you score 39 or 40 with the first 2 darts. This is because you have to leave yourself on 90 or below after all 3 darts to make it a viable shot to take on.

If you go the 19 route and hit two singles with the first 2 darts, you have 116 left. The O/B only brings your score down to 91, so there is no advantage in going this way. In this scenario, throw at a big treble (19 or 20) to bring your score down as much as possible.

155

T20, T19, D19

Although mathematically there are other ways of getting this finish, this is the way to go. Going for it this way doesn't leave a good double, but when you only have one dart at it – especially at the end of a huge finish such as this – it doesn't matter what that double is. Either you get it or you don't. The feelings you get when it goes in is indescribable, and it hurts your opponent deeply.

If your first two darts score 79, you are left with 76, which is straight back for T20 to leave D8. If you can't take it out, the next best thing you can do is to score 139 to leave D8. This is still a huge shot and a perfect setup for the next visit to the board.

If your first dart is single 20, you are left with 135. You can go right back at the T20 to leave 75 with one dart remaining, or T19 to leave 78, or even the bullseye to leave 80 (O/B leaves 110).

Bear in mind that requiring 135 with two darts is a completely different situation than when you have three darts at it. With three darts, the bullseye is the correct shot with the first dart because you are trying to finish it on that turn. With two darts in your hands, it is impossible to finish, and all you want to do is score as much as you can to get your score down to as good a finish as possible when you return to the oche the next time. So in this case, going for the bullseye with the second dart when you require 135 is not the best shot selection. Stay on one of the big trebles and lower your score as much as you can.

If both your first two darts are in single 20, you require 115. This can be T19 to leave 58 when you return, or 96 if you hit single 19. You could also go for another T20 with the last dart to leave 55 when you return, or 95 if all three darts are in single 20.

In the above scenario, if you have scored 40 points with the first two darts, you have to decide for yourself which is the better option: 96 or 95. It may only be one number, but it makes a world of difference to the shot selection.

If you require 96, you have two clear darts at T20 to leave either D18 or D8, depending on whether you get the T20 with the first or second dart. But remember, YOU HAVE to get the treble with one of the first two darts or you cannot finish on that turn. That means that you will need more than 6 darts to finish 155, and that is a recipe for losing the game. Your aim should always be to try to finish the big out-shots in 6 darts or less.

If you require 95, it may seem as though you have left a finish that is not as clean or as simple as leaving 96, and this is true. But what you have done, is to give yourself a great chance of at least having a dart at the bullseye to win the game.

You don't even have to hit a treble. You go for the bullseye with the first dart to leave either 45 or 70. If it's 70, then you throw for T20, D5, or 20, B. Either way, you get a shot at a double on that particular

How To Master The Art Of Finishing

turn, rather than just setting it up for next time and needing more than 6 darts.

I know I am going over old ground again here, but I wanted to emphasize the importance of shot selection, especially when you only have one dart left in your hand. The way you choose to go can change the whole complexion of the game. It's amazing how a difference of even one number can change everything.

Another option with the last dart is to go for the bullseye. This leaves 65 if you hit it, or more importantly, you are left with 90 if you hit the O/B. This is potentially a much better shot than 96 or 95 as described above.

If you are left with 90 on the next turn, you have a chance at D15, D5 or the bullseye, assuming that you start the shot on the 20's. 20, 20, B is potentially a better shot than throwing at 95 or 96, and should be strongly considered if your opponent is in a good position to take the game from you.

If you were wondering what other ways there are to take this shot out, here are a couple of examples. None of them are recommended unless you are doing an exhibition and just want to show off your skills:

T20, T15, B

T18, T17, B

156
T20, T20, D18

This is a favored finish of Raymond van Barneveld, and it is easy to see why. As far as the big finishes goes, this is one of the easier ones to get, although easy should never be associated with any of the bigger finishes.

This shot is all about the T20. If you score 80 with the first two darts, you will require 76, which is T20 again to leave D8 when you return.

If you score 40 with the first two darts, you will be left with 116, which is T20 to leave 56 when you return. If you score 40 with the first two darts, you will be on 116, which is T20 to leave 56 when you return. Score 60 and you will be left on 96 when you return.

As in finish 95 above, you have the option with the last dart to throw at the bullseye. Hitting it would leave 66, but more importantly, hitting the O/B leaves 91, meaning you don't have to get a treble to finish on the next turn. This is something that you have to decide for yourself if it is better for you or not. Both methods are not easy and both options have advantages and disadvantages. Decide for yourself and go for it.

The advanced bullseye technique doesn't apply to this finish because you can't take your score down below 91, but as explained above, there may still be a merit in going this way if you think that 95 gives you a better chance of at least having a dart to win the game.

157

T20, T19, D20

There is only one way to get this finish, and that is T20, T19, and D20. Even the very best miss this more times than they get it. The important thing is to set it up for the next time as best as you can if you can't get it on this turn. That's what the Pro's do almost every time with the big out-shots.

If you score 79 with the first two darts, you are left with 78 with one dart remaining, If the first dart is in single 20, you require 137. Throw again for T20 (or T19 if the T20 is blocked).

Score 80 and you are on 77 with one dart remaining. Throw the last dart at T19. In this case, the worst you should expect is to leave 58 when you return, which is a simple two dart finish.

If you throw the second dart at the T19 after hitting a single 20, you are left on 80. Go back for the T20 to leave D10 when you return.

Even a single 20 leaves 60 when you return, which is a good two dart finish.

If your first two darts are in single 20, you are on 117. Again, this is either T20 or T19. T20 leaves 57 when you return, and T19 leaves 60, both good two dart out-shots.

If you score 60 with all three darts, you are left with 97 when you return. Score 57 and you are on 98. With these options, it is better to throw for the T20 with the last dart and leave 97 than it is to throw for the T19 and leave 98. 97 is a better finish than 98 simply because it potentially gives you a much better double to finish on (D20 as opposed to D19 if you left 98).

Another option, and the better percentage way of throwing the last dart, is to go for the bullseye. If your first two darts are in single 20, you are on 117. If you hit the bullseye, you will need 67 when you return, which is not the best finish to leave, but it is better than leaving 97 or 98.

If you hit the O/B – and this is the main reason why going this way is perhaps the better shot selection – you will be left with 92 when you return. Then you have a chance to finish without hitting a treble. Bullseye leaves 42, and O/B leaves 67. You then throw for T17, D8, or 17, B.

158
T20, T20, D19

Even though there are other ways of getting this finish, this is the way to go for it. In many ways, this is very much like the 155 finish above, but if anything, it is slightly easier because you are not moving to different targets with each dart. *However, please do not confuse easier with easy – this finish is anything but easy!!*

If the first two darts score 80, then you are left with 78 with one dart remaining. T18 would then be your target to leave D12. Single 18 will leave 60 when you return.

If the first dart is in single 20, you are on 138. Stay on the T20. If it goes in, you have scored 80, which is the same scenario as above, leaving you on 78.

If both darts are in single 20, you require 118. You can go for T20 again to leave 58, or single 20 would leave 98. However, in this situation, it is better to throw your last dart at T18. If you get it, you will be left with 64 when you return. If you hit the single – and this is why you should throw for the 18 with the last dart – you will be left with 100 when you return.

100 is a better finish than 98 for many reasons. It is all on the 20's, you are left with a good double (D20), you get two shots at the treble, or you can have two darts at the double if the situation warrants it. So, if you score 40 with the first two darts, go for the 18 with the last one.

If you were wondering what the other methods are for this out-shot, here they are:

You could go for T18, T18, and B. There is absolutely no advantage going for it this way. You have to hit two big trebles, and all you have left yourself is the bullseye. If you have to hit two big trebles to leave a finish, it is far better to leave a double than the bullseye.

The other way is T20, T16, and B. Although this is not a good way to go for the out-shot for the same reasons as above, there is one situation where it might have to be used:

If you start the shot with the normal method, and hit the T20, you will be on 98 with two darts remaining. If the first dart is blocking the treble, or the dart is only just hanging in the board and one more at it will probably knock it out, then assuming your opponent is on a good finish you may be forced to look elsewhere to complete the finish. This is the only time this method becomes viable. Otherwise, stay with the recommended route above.

You do have the option of going for the bullseye with the last dart as well. Rather than leaving yourself on 100 – as you would if you hit single 18 with the last dart, you would leave either 68 if you got the bullseye, or 93 if you got the O/B.

I would argue that in this situation, leaving 100 is better than leaving 93. You may think differently, but you have a better chance of taking out 100 than you do 93, especially if your opponent is on a finish and you are forced to start the shot on the bullseye. Sometimes, leaving a higher number is the better option, and this is one of them.

159

No Finish

You cannot finish 159 with three darts, so unless you have no other choice, don't leave yourself on this number. All you are doing is giving your opponent three extra darts because all you can do from here is set yourself up for the next turn.

160

T20, T20, D20

This isn't the only way to get this finish, but it is the only viable option, unless you are forced to change the shot after the first dart. The top professionals love this finish because it is all on the 20's, and if the first dart goes into the treble, the second dart has a good chance of following it.

If you score 80 with the first two darts, you are left on 80, which is right back at the T20 again to leave D10 when you return.

If the first two darts are in single 20, you go for the T20 again. A 100 will leave you on 60 when you return.

If you score 60 with all three darts, you are on 100 when you return. You could throw the last at the bullseye to leave 95, but for the same reasons as mentioned above, this is not recommended. 100 is a better finish than 95, so stay on the 20's with this out-shot.

There are two occasions when you should consider moving away from the 20's. The first is when your opponent is on a good finish and the first dart is in the T20 and is either blocking it, or is sitting precariously and another dart at it would probably make it fall out.

In this scenario, you are left with 100. You have no choice other than to try for two bull's-eyes. This is a very high risk/high reward shot, and will not work out very often. But if you have no choice, it is better to try and fail rather than just setting it up for a next time that may never happen.

The other occasion is when the first dart is in the single 20, and is blocking the entry to the treble with the second dart. In this case, you are unable to take out the shot on this turn. The best you can do is set it up for the next visit and hope you get a chance to come back to the board.

In this scenario, you are left with 140 and have two darts left in your hands. The T20 bed is blocked. So, what do you do? You throw for the T18. If the first dart goes in, go for it again. If both darts go in the T18, you have left D16 when you return, and you have thrown a really good set of darts.

If the second dart is in T18, and has blocked that treble from another dart, you can throw for the bullseye with the last one. Hit it and you have left D18 when you return. Hit the O/B and you have left 61 when you return.

If the second dart is in single 18, you have left 122 with one dart left in your hand. You can throw again for T18 to leave 68 when you return. Single 18 will leave 104.

You could also throw for the bullseye with the last dart in the above situation. Hit it, and you have left 72 when you return. Hit the O/B, and you have left 97.

The advantage of leaving 97 over 104 is that if you hit the treble (19 in this case) with the first dart, you have two darts at the double. If you had left 104, then even if you hit the treble with the first dart (20 or 18), you still have to waste another dart to leave a double. Always play the percentages whenever you can.

Chapter 11 Quiz

1. You require 151. Your first dart is in T20, and the second lands in single 17. What do you have left? What are you going to do with the last dart? Why?
2. You require 152. The first two darts have scored 80 points. The treble 20 is blocked, and you cannot squeeze another dart in there. What do you have left? What are you going to do with the last dart? Why?
3. You require 153. Your first dart is in single 20, and is a good marker for a second dart to throw back at the T20. You throw for it, and hit the T20. What do you have left? What are you going to do with the last dart? Why?
4. You require 154. What are your options with this shot? Which way are you going to go for it? Why? What do you have left if the first two darts are a single and a treble (20 or 19)? What are you going to do with the last dart? Why?
5. You require 155. Your first two darts are in single 20. What are your options with the third dart? What are you going to do? Why? Why is shot selection with this last dart so important with the finishes from 155-160?
6. You require 156. Your first two darts have scored 40 points. The treble 20 is blocked, and you cannot get another dart in there. What are your options with the last dart? What are you going to do? Why?
7. You require 157. Your first dart is in T20. The second dart is thrown at T19, and hits the single. What do you have left? What are you going to do with the last dart? What would you do if the first two darts landed in single 20? Why?
8. You require 158. Your first two darts are in single 20. What is your shot selection with the last dart? Why is this a better

percentage shot? What does it leave if you get the single of the number you are throwing for?

9. You require 159. Why is leaving this shot always a bad idea? If you were on 259, and the first dart was in the single 20, what would you try to get with the last two darts? Why?

10. You require 160. The first dart is in single 20 and has blocked the treble. What are your options with the next two darts? Why? What would you do with the last dart if the second dart was also in the single of the number you just threw for? Why?

Chapter Twelve: 161-170

In 2000, Ted Hankey famously won the BDO Embassy Lakeside World Championships with a 170 finish against Ronnie Baxter. He won the final 6-0 to crown himself World Champion for the first time. Although he eventually went on to win a second World Title, he will always be remembered for this fantastic achievement, and like Keith Deller before him, he will always be remembered for the amazing finish that won him the world title.

Of course, Deller's finish was 138, and is probably the most famous finish in darts' history, but Hankey's 170 is right up there as one of the greatest finishes of all time.

You have now reached the realm of the big dogs. These are the finishes you see regularly on television when the best players in the world go head to head for the major titles.

At local league level, you may be lucky if you get to see one or two of these finishes in an entire season, and for good reason – they are the hardest ones to get. You need two trebles and a bullseye. There is no other way of getting them. However, when you do get one of these behemoths, you never forget it. It remains a source of pride for the rest of your playing days and beyond.

Number	Solution
161	T20, T17, B T19, T18, B
164	T20, T18, B T19, T19, B
167	T20, T19, B
170	T20, T20, B

Details

There are no finishes for the following numbers, so if at all possible do not leave them. Ever:

162

163

165

166

168

169

Always leave one of the following if you possibly can. You may not get them, but there is always a rush of adrenaline when turning to the oche facing one of these:

161

T20, T17, B – T19, T18, B

Almost all players go for this shot starting on T20. Two-time World Champion Gary Anderson, and more recently 2018 World Champion Rob Cross are two great players who seem to prefer the alternate T19 method.

If the first two darts score 77, you are left with 84, which is right back at T20 again. If you hit it, you have scored 137 to leave 24 when you return. This is a great shot, and the best you can possibly do if you can't take it out on that turn. If the last dart goes into the single 20, you are left on 64 when you return

If the first dart is in single 20, your aim must be to intelligently score as much as you can with the next two darts to leave a good number when you return.

So, if the first dart is in single 20, you are left with 141. Stay on the 20's. If you hit the treble, you have 81 left, which is either T19 or T15, depending on your preference.

Here's the big one with this finish: If the first two darts are in single 20, you have 121 remaining. You could throw at a big treble (20 or 19) to try to leave a good finish when you return. But that is gambling, and you always play the percentages. That is the biggest lesson you have learned from studying the methods in this book.

If you scored 60 with all three darts, you are left with 101 when you return. This is a three dart finish no matter how you go for it (remember, even if you hit T17 with the first dart when you return, you never go for the bullseye when you have two darts in your hands).

It is far better to throw the last dart at the bullseye. If you hit it, you are left with 71 when you return. The percentage shot is when you get the O/B with the last dart. This leaves you on 96 when you come back, and this is massive.

Jim Chatterton

There may only be five points difference between 101 and 96, but in terms of finishing potential, it is huge. 101 is another of those watershed numbers that you need to get below (like 61 in the previous chapters), and by being aware and throwing intelligently at these finishes – especially when you can't take it out and are setting it up for the next visit – you are leveraging the percentages in your favor and giving yourself a much better chance of taking it out on the next turn.

96 is a potential two dart finish, which means you have a chance to give yourself two darts at a double rather than the one that is all you will get by going for 101. You also get two darts at the same treble – 20 – to take out 96.

In this scenario, throwing intelligently trumps going for the glory almost every time, so go for the bullseye with the last dart. Your opponent will probably have no clue why you chose that shot, but because you have studied this book, and have mastered the art of finishing, you know exactly when - *and when not* – to use the bullseye as part of your shot selection, and because you use the board *intelligently*, you set yourself up for the best possible finish in any given situation. And that makes you a very dangerous player indeed, especially if you practice what you have learned diligently, patiently, and regularly.

164

T20, T18, B – T19, T19, B

More and more, players are using the T19 to go for this finish, and it makes sense to do so. If the first dart goes in, you don't have to refocus on a new target with the second dart.

If the first dart is in the treble, and the second one is in single 19, you have scored 76, and are left with 88. The last dart can then be either T20 to leave D14, or T16 to leave D20. Single 20 with the last dart will leave 68 when you return, or single 16 leaves 72.

How To Master The Art Of Finishing

If you watch the top players go for this shot, they often use a creative shot selection to leave themselves on a decent finish if they miss the treble with the first dart. Here's how it works:

If the first dart lands in single 19, the second dart is thrown at the bullseye. If it goes in, you are left with 95. The last dart can be thrown at either T19 or back at the bullseye again to set up the finish for when you return.

If the second dart hits the O/B – and this is the reason why this shot selection is used – throw the last dart at the 20. If it lands in the T20, you are left with 60 when you return. If it goes in the single 20, you are left with 100.

Going for the shot in this manner means you have scored 64, and have rounded your remaining score down to 100. For reasons mentioned in the previous chapters, 100 is a good finish to leave yourself on, and you will have a decent chance of taking it out when you return.

You could also reverse the shot and throw for the 20 with the second dart. In this case, if it goes in the T20, you have scored 79, and are left with 85 remaining. The last dart can then be thrown at either T15 to leave D20 or T19 to leave D14 when you return.

If the second dart is a single 20, throw at the bullseye with the last one. As above, the O/B leaves 100, or the bullseye leaves 75 when you return.

If you decided to go for it with the traditional method of T20, T18, B, and the first dart lands in T20, you obviously throw for the T18 with the second dart. If you hit the single 18, you are left with 86 with one dart remaining. This is T18 again to leave D16 when you return. Single 18 with the last dart will leave 68 when you return.

If the first dart lands in the single 20, you can set the shot up as mentioned above to try to score at least 64 points, and leaving yourself on a decent finish when you return.

If the second dart is then thrown at the T19, and it goes in, you will have scored 77, and will have 87 remaining. The last dart is then thrown at T17 to leave D18 when you return. Single 17 would leave you on 70.

If you hit the single 19 with the second dart, you would be in the same situation as described above, requiring 125 with one dart remaining. The last dart should then be thrown at the bullseye to leave either 100 or 75 when you return.

Of course, there is nothing wrong with setting up the shots in a more traditional manner. If you went the T20 route and hit the single 20 with the first dart, you could stay on the T20 with the second dart. Hit it and you have scored 80 points, leaving 84 with one dart remaining. Hit it again with the last dart for a good 140, and you have left yourself on D12 when you return.

If the first dart is in T20, and the second lands in single 18, you have scored 78 points and have 86 left. The last dart should be right back at T18 to leave D16 when you return. If the T18 is blocked by the second dart, then the bullseye is a good target for the last dart. Hit it, and you will have left D18 when you return. The O/B leaves 61.

If you went the 19 route and didn't want to go the creative route, you could stay on T19 with the second dart. Hit it, and you have scored 76, and as above, you are left on 88 with one dart remaining. T20 leaves D14, or T16 leaves D20.

Another single 19 with the second dart leaves you on 126 with one dart left in your hands. The last dart could be either at the T19 again or T20. T19 would leave you on 69 when you return, or another single 19 leaves 107. T20 with the last dart leaves 66 when you return, or single 20 would leave 106.

167 T20, T19, B

There is only one way to get this monster finish, and that is T20, T19, B. Get this and you'll be doing cartwheels around the dartboard!!

If the first dart is in T20 and the second lands in single 19, you have scored 79, and are left with 88 (do you see the patterns again here?). As above, you have the option with the last dart of either T16 to leave D20, or T20 to leave D14 when you return. Single 16 leaves 72, and single 20 leaves 68.

If the first dart lands in the single 20, you require 147. T20 would leave 87, which is T17 with the last dart. Hit it, and you have made a great shot of 131 to leave D18 when you return. Single 17 would leave 70.

If both the first two darts are in single 20, you are then left on 127. Throw again for the T20 to try to score as much as you can. Scoring 100 would leave you on 67 when you return. Score 60 with all three darts and you are left with 107 when you return.

If the first two darts are blocking the T20, throw the last one at T19. The two single 20's left you on 127, so T19 would leave 70 when you return. Single 19 would leave 108.

If the first dart is in single 20, and is blocking the treble, throw the second dart at T19. Single 20 left you on 147, and T19 would then leave 90. The last dart would then be either T18 to leave D18, or bullseye to leave D20 when you return. Single 18 leaves 72 or O/B leaves 65.

If the second dart is in single 19, you would have scored 39 points and be left with 128. The last one could be at either T19 again, or T18. T19 with the last dart would leave 71 when you return, or T18 would leave 74. Single 19 again leaves 109, and single 18 leaves 110.

170

T20, T20, B

During the 2016 PDC UK Open Darts Championships, the defending champion and world number one Michael van Gerwen seemed to defy all the laws of probability when in successive matches he hit not just one, but two 170 finishes!

Not just that, but in the first match he did it in, he scored an incredible 18 perfect darts live on television – which was the second time he has done this as well. He ended one leg with 6 perfect darts, scoring 177, and then taking out 170. That's taking out 347 in 6 darts!

The next leg was even better – he hit 180, 180, and 141 for a perfect 9 dart game. This gave him 15 perfectly thrown darts back to back. He then opened the next leg with yet another 177, making 18 consecutive darts thrown with pure perfection. Just to add the icing to the cake, he then went on to finish 170 yet again in that leg.

MVG (as he is known), is currently riding the crest of the wave as I write this book. He recently broke the world record three dart average for a live TV match in the Premier League against Michael Smith. His final average was 123.4, and if it wasn't for a few missed doubles at the end it would have been even higher.

The 170 finish is the big one, the finish that every player wants to hit at least once in their playing career. There is no greater feeling than hitting this finish at a key point in a match. Most players never get to experience this feeling because it is such a massive shot, but if anything, it is slightly easier than the 167 out-shot because there is no moving all over the dartboard when taking it out. This shot is all about the T20, and if you hit two of them with the first two darts, it becomes a psychological battle in your own mind when you go for the bullseye, because you know that this is the biggest of them all.

If the first two darts score 80 points, you are left on 90 with one dart remaining. The last dart is then thrown either at T18 to leave D18, or the bullseye to leave D20 when you return. Single 18 leaves 72 or the O/B leaves 65.

Two single 20's leaves 130 and you should remain on the T20 with the last dart if it isn't blocked from the first two. Scoring 100 leaves you 70 when returning to the oche.

If the T20 is blocked with the second dart, throw the last one at T18. If it goes in, you have left 76 when you return. Single 18 will leave 112.

The same is true if the first dart is in single 20. If the treble is blocked, use the 18's with the next two darts. T18 with the second dart leaves 98. Normally this would be T20, but as it is blocked in this scenario, throw again for the T18 (assuming that isn't also blocked). T18 again would leave you on 42, and this 128 score would be a very good shot in these circumstances.

Single 18 with the second dart would leave 132 with one dart remaining. You could then go either back at the T18 or the bullseye. T18 would leave 78 when you return, or single 18 would leave 114. The bullseye with the last dart would leave 82, or the O/B would leave 107.

Chapter 12 Quiz

1. You require 161. Your first dart goes in T20, and the second lands in single 17. What do you have left? What are you going to do with the last dart? Why?
2. You require 161. The first two darts are both in the single 20. What are your options with the last dart? What is your shot selection going to be? Why?
3. You require 164. You decide to go the T19 route, and the first dart hits the T19. The second dart goes in the single 19. What do you have left? What are you going to do with the last dart? Why?
4. You require 164. The first dart lands in single 19. What are your options with the last two darts? What can you do to leave yourself a decent finish without having to hit a treble? What are you going to do? Why?
5. You require 164. The first dart lands in T20. The second dart goes into the single 18. What do you have left? What are you going to do with the last dart? Why?
6. You require 167. Your first two darts are in single 20 and T20, scoring 80 points. What are you going to do with the last dart? Why?
7. You require 167. You hit the T20 with the first dart. You aim the second one at T19, but it misses to the left and goes into T7. What do you have left? What are you going to do with the last dart? Why?
8. You require 170. The first two darts are in T20 and single 20. What are you going to do with the last dart? Why?
9. You require 170. The first two darts are in single 20. What are you going to do with the last dart? Why? What would you do if the T20 was blocked by the first two darts? Why? What would your shot selection leave you on when you return?
10. You are on 170. The first dart is in single 20 and it has blocked the treble. What are you going to do with the last two darts?

> Why? What will your shot selection leave you on when you return?

These are all very difficult out-shots, but when you operate at this level nothing is going to be easy. Although the aim is to take out the big shots in six darts or less, do not be discouraged if you don't manage to do it, especially at first. These finishes require a large amount of skill, and this can only come after countless hours of practice and frustration.

Depending on your aspirations, keep at it and eventually all the hard work and dedication will pay off. When the final bullseye goes in at the end of a 170 finish to win a tight match, every minute of all the hard work you have put in will have been worth it.

Jim Chatterton

Conclusion

Congratulations on reaching the end of this book. You have demonstrated a level of commitment and dedication few will manage, and you will reap the rewards for the remainder of your playing career.

The road has been a long one, with many twists and turns along the way. There have been some major road blocks and brick walls where you stumbled and fell, but every time you picked yourself up, reminded yourself why you took on this arduous task in the first place, and got back on the saddle.

By doing this, you have already elevated yourself to a level far beyond the norm, and you now have the knowledge – not only of how to finish, but more importantly about yourself and your strength of character, to take on and master difficult tasks -to take this as far as your desire and skills allow.

By diligently studying every chapter in this book, you will have mastered the following concepts:

- You will have mastered the 3-step process to becoming a master of darts finishing
- You will have learnt that every finish builds on the ones below. By knowing every combination of the finishes from the bottom up, learning becomes a step by step process that removes all guesswork and confusion.
- You know the importance of always knowing what you have remaining, no matter where the dart lands.
- Because you always know what you have remaining, and because you are armed with in-depth knowledge of every

finish below the one you are at, then you always know what to throw for, even if the dart misses its intended target.

- You know the important differences between being faced with a finish with 2 darts in your hands and the same one when you have all three in your hands.
- You always play the percentages on every out-shot.
- You understand when – *and when not* – to utilize the bullseye as a part of your shot selection.
- You understand when throwing for a double-double finish is the right way to go, and is the best use of the percentages.
- You will never again be confused when going for any finish – no matter what you hit. You will always instantly know what to do and where to throw.

By reaching the end of the book you have mastered the three-step process, and you have now graduated to the fourth and final step – Mathematical Enlightenment. You have reached the stage where mathematics is no longer required. You know instinctively what to go for every time, no matter the situation.

You have now joined the small percentage of players worldwide who never struggle with knowing where to aim their darts. The big issue for you now is being able to hit them consistently, and that requires countless hours of dedicated practice. If you show the same levels of fortitude with your practice as you have with mastering this book, you will be able to take your game to heights you never believed possible, and that, at the end of the day, is the ultimate goal.

I wish you the very best of luck, wherever you play and whatever your ultimate goal. Armed with the information inside this book, you will be a very formidable opponent indeed….

P.S. Don't forget to check out the extra resources and articles that can be found at *http://dartsfinishing.com/*

Bonus Chapter – Finishing Routines and Practice Games

A good practice routine contains the following characteristics:

- It is measurable, and allows you to track your progress
- It allows you to "Drill Down" on whatever part of your game you want to work on.
- It is interesting and enjoyable
- It is challenging, but not so much that it puts you off.
- It has intensity, and makes you try with each and every dart

With the exception of the warm-up routine that I include here as it can also be used as a stand-alone practice session when time is short, the remainder of the routines in this chapter contains the above 5 points.

If you vary your practice, it keeps it interesting and prevents you from becoming stale. The ultimate goal of any practice session is to improve your game, and every routine in this chapter will help you attain that goal. None of these are easy, but they can be scaled up or down depending on your skill level and how much time you have available.

They are also designed to simulate match-play as much as possible. Some of these routines will have your palms sweating and will see your anxiety levels increase as you get close to completing them. There will also be the feelings of frustration, because you will miss a shot and have to start all over again.

Do not allow frustration to set in when practicing, and take frequent breaks if needed. These sessions will not only improve your darts game beyond recognition, but they will also greatly improve your match-play temperament if you keep at it and control the frustrations as they arise.

Do this on a regular basis and your confidence and skill level will explode, and you will approach every game with a locked in, laser-like focus and intensity, no matter who you are playing, or whatever the situation. You will be ready.

So, without further ado, here are the practice routines:

Warm-Up Routine

This is the same routine that was demonstrated at the start of the book. It is great for not only warming up, but can also be used as a standalone routine in itself. If you are short of time, it is a great little session that can get your arm going, give you good practice at every double on the board, and can be as intensive as you want by trying to hit as many consecutive doubles as possible and breaking your previous records.

You are now going to hit every double twice, but with a twist. You could just go around the board from 1 to 20, hit the bull and come back to 1, and that would work just fine. However, you are practicing for the game of 501 (or any 01 game), so it makes sense to practice with this in mind.

Rather than go around the board linearly, you are going to start at D20, and then throw as you would in a proper game. So next you throw at D10, and then D5. This gets you used to throwing the same way as you would in a match-play situation and gives you an edge because you are always used to throwing at doubles in the same manor.

So, you get to D5, then what? Well, then you have gotten as far as you can get in this segment, so you come back up again. You hit D5, D10, and then D20. You always go as far as the breakdown of that number allows before coming back up again.

How To Master The Art Of Finishing

Next you move onto D19. As this does not break down you hit it twice (it doesn't have to be in the same throw, although that is always nice to do). Then it is the turn of the 18's, and you hit D18, D9, D9 and then D18 again. This may look complicated at first, but it is easy once you have done it a time or two,

Continue in this manor until you reach D11. Again, you hit two of those and then the outer ring of doubles is done. It is now time for the bullseye, and this time you have to hit two of the red, center bulls. The red bull is double the green ring (25 points), and is the highest double you can finish on. It is also the most difficult, and it comes into play a lot more as you get into the higher finishing combinations.

For clarity, the doubles warm up routine is shown in the table below. If time allows, always complete this before moving onto the actual finishes. The more you can practice hitting the doubles the better you will be when it comes to the real thing.

20	10	5	5	10	20				
19	19								
18	9	9	18						
17	17								
16	8	4	2	1	1	2	4	8	16
15	15								
14	7								
13	13								
12	6	3	3	6	12				

11	11							
B	B							

At first this may take a while to complete, but don't give up. Mastering the art of finishing is as difficult as it gets in the game of darts, and the more you practice the easier it will get. As a rough guide, eventually the entire sequence detailed above will take you no more than 15-20 minutes once you reach a good level. If you can do it faster than that then you are a very formidable player indeed!

Bob's 29

This routine was, or at least I think it was, originally invented by 1988 World Champion Bob Anderson. It is a fantastic practice routine that is as rewarding as it is frustrating. And it is extremely addictive.

You start with an odd number. I stated 29 in the title above, but it can be any number you feel comfortable with. If you are just starting out, then start on a higher number of 51 or even more. Once you beat it, lower the starting number until you reach the 25-95 area. Then you will be hitting the doubles like a Pro!!

Here's how it works:

You start with the odd number you allocated to yourself at the beginning. You then throw all 3 darts at each double in turn, starting at 1 and going all the way to 20 and then the bullseye (it has to be the red bullseye).

So, you start on D1. You add whatever you hit to the total score, so let's say you hit one double 1 out of the 3 darts. You add 2 points to your score of 29 (or whatever you started out with), putting you on 31. If you hit two doubles you would add 4 points, or 6 if you hit all three.

If you miss with all 3 darts, you then have to subtract the value of that double from your overall score. In this instance, you started with 29 points. You miss all 3 darts at D1, so you subtract 2 points from the total, leaving you on 27 points.

You then move on to D2 and repeat the process. If you hit one double out of the 3 darts, you add 4 points to your score, and if you hit 2 doubles you add 8 points, and 12 if you hit all 3. If you miss with all 3 darts, you subtract the value of the double from your score – in this case 4 points. Then you repeat the process on D3, D4, D5 and so on.

Now here's the part which makes this game so addictive: If your score goes below zero then you have lost the game. You are out and have to start again at D1.

You will be amazed at the number of times you get as far as D18, D19 or D20 – or even the bullseye – before losing the game. It's arguably the best practice routine for hitting the doubles ever invented, and a lot of credit has to go to Bob Anderson for sharing it with the world.

When you first begin this practice routine, just being able to complete it will be an achievement in itself. But for reference purposes, and these are just my own humble opinions, a score in the 100+ range is a good average score. 200+ is a good, solid score, and 300+ is really getting up there as a very good score. If you can get over 400 you are doing extremely well, and anything above 600 is elite level.

Good luck with this routine. I think you will enjoy it, and it will become a challenge all of itself. Don't despair if you are just starting out and struggle to finish the game. Raise the starting number and go from there. Lower it once you can complete it at the higher number. Once you reach 27, stick with it and see how high you can get with the scores.

2-100 (3 Darts)

This is a great practice game that can be spread out over several different sessions. It is also the one I recommend for really getting the finishes ingrained in your head and learning them deeply and completely.

The finishes you will encounter here represent every finish you will ever encounter for the vast majority of your playing career, no matter what standard you eventually reach. You will find yourself facing a finish between 2-100 most of the time, which is why it is so important you practice them as often as possible.

This routine will - *once-and-for-all* - solve all the problems that arise when your darts miss their intended targets. By regularly incorporating this routine in your practice sessions, you will encounter every scenario that is possible with every finish, and after you have done them a few times, you will know what to go for without even thinking about it.

This routine -allied to the detailed finishing theory contained within the pages of this book – will take you effortlessly and easily to step 4 – Mathematical Enlightenment. For this reason, this is a highly recommended routine to incorporate into you regular practice sessions.

Not only does it ingrain every finish into your brain easily and effortlessly, it is also a brilliant way to add intensity to your practice by forcing you to try with every dart. Just like in real match-play, you will feel the tension when you're throwing. You will have to handle the frustration that arises when you miss, and you will have to remain calm under pressure to complete the shot. And it gets harder the further you go into the routine.

This is a fantastic routine to practice every finish on the board from 2-100, so don't overlook it. It's certainly not easy, but the rewards are huge. Once you see yourself regularly hitting all these finishes with 3 darts or less, your confidence will soar, and it will take your game to places you never believed possible.

If you are just starting out, don't despair. Like all the routines included in this bonus chapter, it is adjustable to your current level of play. Start out with 6, 9, or even more darts to get each finish. Once you can do it, lower the number of darts needed until you can do them all in 3. This way, even if you are a complete newcomer, you will knock years off the learning curve and you will improve at an incredible rate.

Although it is simple in concept, this routine is far from easy.

Here's how it works:

Starting on D1, cycle through every single finish one at a time with three darts or less (or whatever your starting number is). The aim is to go all the way from 2-100, hitting every single one of them along the way.

This routine can take a while to get through, but it can be broken up into manageable sessions. It doesn't matter if it takes one hour, one day, one week or longer. Just stay with it and get there. You will learn so much by doing this, and you will get intimate with every single one of the finishes.

You have to hit the finish with 3 darts or less or you don't move on. Give it a try. It is difficult and addictive, but the rewards are huge if you persevere with it.

The early ones are easy. You get all 3 darts at D1. If you hit single 1 you have burst your score, so start again with all 3 darts.

Then you move onto 3. This is a two-dart finish, so you only get 2 darts to hit the double. Then you are back to getting all three darts again when you go for D2, and so on.

Even when you get into the 41-50 range and the 51-60's, you still have 2 darts to get the double. Once you get to 61 and above, it starts to get harder.

When you get past 80 it starts to get really difficult, especially in the 90's. 99 is a special finish all by itself because it is the only one from the entire routine that is a 3 dart finish. Once you reach 100 congratulate yourself on a job well done, because you will deserve it. Then go back and do it again.

This routine is a lesson in patience, but it is well worth the effort you put into it. Let's move on…

101-170 (6 Darts)

This is an advanced routine, and is the partner to the one above, and it steps it up yet another notch. This routine takes you all the way up to the coveted 170, and if you do this after completing the previous one, you will have gotten to hit every single finish on the dartboard. Not many players can ever say they have done that!

This routine follows the same patterns as the previous one except that this time you give yourself 6 darts to complete the task. If you are just getting started, you might want to skip this until you can complete the other ones presented in this chapter. If you still want to attempt it, raise the number of darts required from 6 to whatever you need. It could be 12, 15, or even 18. It doesn't matter at the beginning. As your skill and knowledge improves, lower the number of darts needed until you are able to cycle through it in 6 darts or less. You will then be a really feared and formidable finisher!

As before, this routine can be split over several sessions. After the first 3 darts, you will find yourself more often than not on one of the finishes in the previous routine. This will give you more practice at the finishes in the critical range of 2-100, whilst giving you a chance of hitting the big, adrenaline pumping dream out-shots.

Once you reach 170 with 6 darts or less, you can either start again at 101, or start at the very beginning with the previous routine and go all the way from 2-170 in either 3 or 6 darts. This is difficult, but incredibly rewarding.

170

This is a great practice game where you give yourself a set amount of darts to hit 170. This routine will give you plenty of practice on different finishes, depending on what you leave yourself after each turn, and of course you get to throw at the big one every time you start. When you hit it, especially for the first time, the feeling is ethereal.

If you practice this solo, give yourself a set amount of darts to hit the finish. If you don't get it within the specified number of darts, go back to 170 and start again.

If you are just starting out, give yourself 12, 15, or even 18 darts to get this finish. As your skill and confidence increases, lower the number of darts to around 9. This will give you a lot of practice on many different finishing combinations, and it will help immensely in learning the finishes so that you won't even need to look at the book or any out-shot chart ever again.

This is also a great game for practicing with other players. If there are two or even three of you, take it in turns to go for this finish. If there are two of you, you still have 9 darts to hit the finish. Let's say that you and a friend are practicing this routine:

You throw first at 170. You score 60 points. Your partner has to try to finish 110 with his 3 darts. He scores 54 points (20, 18, 16), to leave 56 after 6 darts. You then return to the board to take out 56 with either 2 or 3 darts. Your partner then starts the whole routine again, throwing at 170 with his first set of 3 darts.

Let's say that you missed the 56 finish, leaving 20 after 9 darts. Because you only had 9 darts to complete the routine, then regardless of what score you left, your partner starts the whole routine again when he comes back to the board.

By practicing in this manner, it gives both of you the opportunity to throw for a big out-shot, as well as a good 1 or 2 dart finish, and more importantly, it gives both of you plenty of practice at setting up finishes for the next shot, which is hugely important.

If there are three of you playing, then each of you takes one throw each to finish 170. Once you successfully complete it, rotate who starts the routine so you each get to throw at different combinations and all three different components of this practice routine:

- The big 170
- The setup shot
- Finishing from within the "Hot Zone" of 2-80

If there are more than three of you, then it is probably better to practice a different routine, of which there are plenty to choose from.

This is a great routine that should be a regular part of your practice. If you play in enough tournaments, you will see players of all standards practicing this game together all the time. It's a great warm-up routine, it gets your arm going, and it gets you thinking about - and throwing for – the important doubles and finishes. Make sure this routine is a part of YOUR routine.

Painting by Numbers

I don't know the names of some of these routines because they are one's I have developed myself over the years. I don't lay claim to inventing them – I am sure there are many different variations of these routines being practiced all over the world, but I have never personally seen them published anywhere before, so I created my own rules as I went along.

The one thing I never did was to give them a name, so please forgive me for the names I have adopted for them. As I said, you may know the routine under a different name, and if so, please feel free to use the one's you already know.

How To Master The Art Of Finishing

This routine is a great practice session for two or more players. Here's how it works:

The aim is to go around the board on every double from 1 to 20, then the bullseye, and then going all the way back down to D1, finishing once again on the bullseye.

If you hit one or more doubles on each turn, you continue until you miss with all 3 darts. Then your opponents have their turn.

So, let's say that you win the cork and start the game. Your first dart misses, the second dart goes in D1, and the third dart misses D2. You hit one or more with the 3 darts, so you continue. Your next 3 darts are a perfect set; you hit D2, D3, and D4.

You give yourself a pat on the back and continue. However, you miss all three darts at D5. So, your turn has ended, and your opponent begins his turn.

Unfortunately, he/she misses the D1 with all three darts, so you return to resume your turn. You then go for D5 again, and so on.

Once you get to D20, you have to hit the red bullseye, and then go straight back for D20. Continue backwards down the doubles until you reach D1. The game ends when the first player hits the red bullseye.

If time is short you can shorten the game to just one round of doubles and the bullseye, but otherwise go both up and down the doubles so you hit both of them twice.

It's a great routine that makes you try with every single dart. Many times, a player can come back from being way behind with a good run on the doubles. The ultimate aim is to go around the board without missing a turn, but this is very difficult to achieve. The good thing is that players of all levels can play this game, and as long as you are evenly matched it can be a very exciting game to be involved in.

Jim Chatterton

Around the Board without Missing

This is a game that the great John Part introduced. John is a three-time World Champion, and is widely recognized as being one of the greatest players of all time. He can certainly lay claim to be the greatest player ever from North America.

This is a very difficult routine that should only be attempted by advanced players. If you are able to complete this practice session, you are one heck of a player that everyone else should be looking out for.

Here's how it works:

Starting on D1, you have to go around the board, hitting every double along the way. Adding the bullseye at the end is optional. Just reaching D20 in this game is an achievement in itself, so adding the bullseye is a personal choice.

You have to hit one or more doubles on each and every turn. If you miss with all 3 darts, the game is lost, and you have to start again at D1.

There are no awards for hitting three doubles in three darts, you just keep going. Let's say you start and hit D1 with the first dart. The second dart is thrown at D2. It misses, so you throw again at D2, which misses again.

Because you hit a double on that turn (D1), you continue with the game. You throw at D2. If you get it, you move onto D3, D4 and so on. Every double has to be hit just one time before moving on to the next one.

As soon as you miss with all 3 darts, the game is over, and you go back to D1. As previously stated, this is an incredibly difficult game to complete. When you get near the end, the adrenaline starts to flow, and the same tensions you get in match-play begin to emerge. You know you are so close, and one mistake can cost you the game.

How To Master The Art Of Finishing

When you get as far as D18 and miss, the frustrations and disappointments are very real, especially as you know you have to go right back to D1 and start again.

This routine can be adapted to allow for some errors, but that is covered in the routine above called Painting by Numbers. If you want to adapt this one, perhaps you could narrow the field down somewhat by only having to hit a certain number of doubles on each session.

For instance, you could have a session where you have to go from D1 to D5. Once you do that, move onto the next set of five etc. Whichever way you decide to go with this, it is a fantastic practice routine to have in your armory, especially for advanced tournament players.

2/3 Darts in Each Double

This routine is not only great for doubles practice, but also for grouping (which is very important in the scoring phase of the game). The idea is to go around the board in order from D1 to D20, and then the bullseye.

Along the way, you have to put 2 out of three darts in each double before moving on. There are no penalties with this game (unless you choose to add them), and if you fail to put 2/3 in a double, you keep throwing at it until you do. Then, and only then do you move onto the next one.

This may seem a bit daunting at first, especially for newer players, but persevere with this one because you will be surprised at how well it comes together. Once you start hitting them, your confidence soars, and you realize that you CAN do this.

You will be putting 2/3 in the doubles with regularity, and it will lift your entire game. Suddenly, you are following a dart in the T20 with another one; It will change your game forever.

Round the Board

This is a routine that should be in everyone's practice regimen. It's a great warm-up, and can also be used as a standalone session by itself. It is very similar to the warm-up routine I explained at the beginning of this book, as well as again at the start of this chapter. The big difference is that this routine is to be done linearly, and doesn't follow the finishing patterns of a 501 game.

This is a game that can be measured to monitor your progress over the weeks and months ahead. Starting at D1, go around the board hitting every double from D1 to D20, and then the bullseye. Keep a count of the number of darts it took you to complete the task, and see if you can break your record. By doing this it becomes competitive, and you will try as hard as you can with each and every dart. And that is how you improve.

Once you have gone up the board in doubles, start again at D20 and go all the way back down to D1 before finishing on the bullseye. Again, keep a count of how many darts it takes you to complete it and try to break your records.

101 (6)

This is a brilliant routine for practicing combination finishing. Give yourself 6 darts (or more if you are just starting out), and try to finish 101. If you can do it in 3 darts (or 2 if you really want to go for it that way), then great, but the majority of the time you will be doing it within 6 darts rather than 3.

You will get plenty of practice on the big trebles, and you will throw a lot at different parts of the board to setup your shots at the finish. It will also help to ingrain the finishes you encounter, and it will cement them into your brain, so you won't even have to think about them anymore – you will just know instinctively what they are.

This can also be a good two-person routine. You can rotate who starts the shot so you both get practice on different aspects of the finish. It always feels good being the one who takes out the 101 out-shot!

201

This is a very good game for both scoring, finishing, and setting up your finishes. It is one of the best practice routines you can do, and as such you should use it often.

There are two ways to approach this, so you can mix it up and keep it interesting.

The first method is to give yourself as many darts as it takes to finish the 201. Once you have done it, try to beat it on the next turn. Keep doing this over and over, and see well you can do it. If you can do it in 9 darts or less consistently you will be a very dangerous player.

The other method is to give yourself a set number of darts to finish the 201. 9 darts are the optimum, but it can be set at whatever level you are currently at. If you are a beginner, set it at 15, 18, or even 21 darts if you want to. You will be amazed at how fast you will progress if you are serious about it.

9 darts are the optimum for this routine. As I stated above, if you can consistently take out 201 in 9 darts or less you are a very capable player indeed.

100 to 130

Following on from the 101 routine above, this routine takes it a step further and gives you practice at a whole plethora of finishes.

Give yourself 6 darts (or 9, 12, or even 15 if you are just starting out), and go for the 100 finish. If you hit it, you move up by one. So, then you go for 101. If you miss with 6 darts (or more), you go back a number. Once you reach 130 the game is over, and you start again or move onto a different routine.

Conversely, set yourself a low number as well. 80 is a good number that gives you a great range of finishes to go for. If you reach this low number, the game is lost, and you start again.

This is not as easy as it looks, and it will give you some great practice on many different finishing combinations. It will also get you used to actually hitting these out-shots, and you will begin to feel comfortable when you are faced with them in a match-play situation. It's a state of mind, and when you are hitting them every day in your home practice routines, you begin to expect to hit them when it counts, and that is the winning mindset you are trying to cultivate with your practice.

32 and up

This is a good routine that will give you plenty of practice on the finishes in the hot zone. You will spend the vast majority of your playing career going for finishes within this range, and for this reason, these are the most important finishes you will ever learn or practice. Get these down and you will move ahead of 90% of the darts players out there.

The Hot Zone as I like to call it, incorporates every finish from 2-80. This routine takes a subset of these and really drills them down. Here's how it works:

Starting at 32 (you can, of course, change this to whatever starting number you desire), give yourself two throws to get the finish. If you hit it within the two throws, you move on to the next number and repeat all the way to 80. If you miss with the two throws, you go back a number.

This gets increasingly more difficult the further you get, so players new to the game initially might want to give themselves more than just two throws.

Like the routine above, set yourself a low number as well. If you hit this target you have lose the game and start again. A good starting number is 20.

If you are an advanced player, you do this routine with just one throw rather than two. This makes it a very tough routine, and as you get nearer the finishing mark of 80, the same tensions that you experience in regular match-play will arise. This makes it a great practice routine to add to your repertoire.

Fast Vinny's 121-150

Dutch professional player Vincent van der Vort has a couple of great routines he shared with the world. Naturally, these are difficult and advanced routines, but if you can get them down your game will improve exponentially.

In this routine, Vincent starts on 121 and gives himself 9 darts to get it. If he gets it, he moves on to 122 and so on, all the way up to 150.

Here's the kicker – If he misses the finish within the allocated 9 darts he goes all the way back down to 121 and starts all over again.

For newer players, or anyone that finds this routine outside of their level of abilities, there is nothing wrong with increasing the amount of darts you need to be competitive with it. Ultimately, your goal should be to reach the stage where you can tackle this routine and give it your best efforts to complete it with 9 darts or less. Good luck!!

Fast Vinny's 40 down to 2

Another tough routine that Vincent practices regularly is to go for the following sequence of shots:

40, 36, 32, 24, 20, 16, 12, 8, 4, 2.

Here's how it works:

You have 3 darts at each finish. Starting at 40, you have to go all the way down the sequence hitting every double within the 3 darts. If you miss you go back to 40 and start again.

Once you can do this on a fairly regular basis, you can drop the number of darts to two. If you are a very advanced player, you can try it with just 1 dart at each double, which is probably what Vincent does. If you can do this, then you are at a professional level, and you will be playing in the elite circles of the game.

Even though I have added a good number of practice routines in this chapter, there are many, many more you can choose from. Do a search online and you will find lots of suggestions for your practice. If none of these work for you, then make up your own!

Don't forget to check out *www.DartsFinishing.com* for further articles and resources.

Good luck and best wishes!!

Jim Chatterton

Appendix

Complete Out-shot Chart

Number	Solution
2	D1
3	1, D1
4	D2
5	1, D2 3, D1
6	D3 2, D2
7	3, D2
8	D4
9	1, D4
10	D5 2, D4
11	3, D4
12	D6 4, D4
13	5, D4

14	D7 6, D4
15	7, D4 3, D6
16	D8
17	1, D8 9, D4
18	D9 2, D8
19	3, D8 11, D4
20	D10
21	5, D8 13, D4 1, D10
22	D11 6, D8 2, D10
23	7, D8 3, D10
24	D12 8, D8 4, D10

25	9, D8 17, D4 1, D12 5, D10
26	D13 10, D8 2, D12 6, D10
27	11, D8 3, D12 19, D4 7, D10
28	D14 12, D8 4, D12 8, D10
29	13, D8 5, D12 9, D10
30	D15 14, D8 6, D12 10, D10
31	15, D8 7, D12 11, D10
32	D16

33	1, D16 17, D8 9, D12 13, D10
34	D17 2, D16 10, D12 14, D10
35	3, D16 19, D8 11, D12 15, D10
36	D18
37	5, D16 1, D18 13, D12 17, D10
38	D19 6, D16 2, D18 14, D12 18, D10
39	7, D16 3, D18 15, D12 19, D10
40	D20

41	9, D16 1, D20 5, D18 17, D12
42	10, D16 2, D20 6, D18 18, D12
43	11, D16 3, D20 7, D18 19, D12
44	12, D16 4, D20 8, D18 20, D12
45	13, D16 5, D20 9, D18
46	14, D16 6, D20 10, D18
47	15, D16 7, D20 11, D18
48	16, D16 8, D20 12, D18

49	17, D16 9, D20 13, D18
50	18, D16 10, D20 14, D18 B
51	19, D16 11, D20 15, D18
52	20, D16 12, D20 16, D18
53	13, D20 17, D18
54	14, D20 18, D18
55	15, D20 19, D18
56	16, D20 20, D18
57	17, D20 O/B, D16
58	18, D20
59	19, D20

60	20, D20
61	O/B, D18 T15, D8 T7, D20 11, B T11, D14
62	T10, D16 T14, D10 T18, D4 12, B T12, D13
63	T13, D12 T17, D6 T9, D18 13, B
64	T16, D8 T8, D20 14, B T14, D11
65	O/B, D20 T15, D10 T11, D16 T19, D4 15, B
66	T10, D18 B, D8 T14, D12 16, B T16, D9

67	T17, D8 T9, D20 17, B
68	T20, D4 T12, D16 T16, D10 18, B T18, D7
69	T15, D12 T19, D6 T11, D18 19, B
70	T18, D8 T10, D20 20, B T20, D5
71	T13, D16 T17, D10
72	T16, D12 T12, D18 T20, D6
73	T19, D8 T11, D20
74	T14, D16 T18, D10
75	T17, D12 T13, D18

	O/B, B
76	T20, D8 T12, D20
77	T19, D10 T15, D16
78	T18, D12 T14, D18
79	T19, D11 T13, D20
80	T20, D10 T16, D16
81	T19, D12 T15, D18
82	B, D16 T14, D20
83	T17, D16
84	T20, D12 T16, D18
85	T15, D20 T19, D14
86	T18, D16 B, D18
87	T17, D18
88	T20, D14

	T16, D20
89	T19, D16
90	T20, D15 T18, D18 B, D20
91	T17, D20 B, 9, D16 O/B, 16, B O/B, T16, D9
92	T20, D16 B, 10, D16 O/B, 17, B O/B, T17, D8
93	T19, D18 B, 11, D16 B, 3, D20 O/B, 18, B O/B, T18, D7
94	T18, D20 B, 12, D16 O/B, 19, B O/B, T19, D6
95	T19, D19 B, 13, D16 O/B, 20, B O/B, T20, D5
96	T20, D18

97	T19, D20
98	T20, D19
99	T19, 10, D16 T17, 16, D16
100	T20, D20
101	T19, 12, D16 19, B, D16 19, T14, D20 T20, 9, D16 T20, 1, D20 20, T19, D12 T17, B
102	T20, 10, D16 T20, 2, D20 20, B, D16 20, T14, D20
103	T20, 3, D20 T20, 11, D16 20, T17, D16 T19, 14, D16 T19, 6, D20 T19, 10, D18 19, T20, D12 19, T16, D18
104	T20, 12, D16 T20, 4, D20 20, T20, D12 20, T16, D18

	T18, 18, D16 T16, 16, D20 T18, B
105	T19, 16, D16 T19, 8, D20 19, T18, D16 T20, 13, D16 T20, 5, D20 20, T15, D20 20, T19, D14
106	T20, 14, D16 T20, 6, D20 T20, 10, D18 20, T18, D16
107	T19, 18, D16 T19, 10, D20 19, T20, D14 19, T16, D20 T19, B T20, 15, D16 T20, 7, D20 20, T17, D18
108	T20,16, D16 T20, 8, D20 20, T20, D14 20, T16, D20 T19, 19, D16 T18, 18, D18 T17, 17, D20
109	T20, 17, D16

	T20, 9, D20
	20, T19, D16
	T19, 20, D16
	T19, 12, D20
	19, T18, D18
	19, B, D20
110	T20, 18, D16
	T20, 10, D20
	20, T18, D18
	20, T20, D15
	20, B, D20
	T20, B
111	T20, 19, D16
	T20, 11, D20
	20, T17, D20
	T19, 14, D20
	T19, 18, D18
	19, T20, D16
112	T20, 20, D16
	T20, 12, D20
	T18, 18, D20
113	T20, 13, D20
	T20, 17, D18
	20, T19, D18
	T19, 16, D20
	T19, 20, D18
	19, T18, D20
114	T20, 14, D20
	T20, 18, D18
	20, T18, D20

115	T19, 18, D20 19, T20, D18 T20, 15, D20 20, T19, D19
116	T20, 16, D20 T20, 20, D18 T19, 19, D20
117	T20, 17, D20 20, T19, D20 T19, 20, D20 19, T20, D19
118	T20, 18, D20 20, T20, D19
119	T19, T10, D16 T19, T14, D10 T19, 12, B 19, T20, D20
120	T20, 20, D20
121	T20, 11, B T20, T11, D14 20, T17, B T17, 20, B T17, T20, D5 17, T18, B T20, O/B, D18 T20, T15, D8 T17, T18, D8 B, T13, D16 B, T17, D10

122	T18, 18, B T18, T18, D7 O/B, T19, D20
123	T19, 16, B T19, T16, D9 19, T18, B
124	T20, 14, B T20, T14, D11 20, T18, B
125	O/B, T20, D20 B, T17, D12 B, O/B, B T15, D20, D20 15, T20, B
126	T19, 19, B T19, T19, D6
127	T20, 17, B T20, T17, D8 20, T19, B
128	T18, T18, D10 T18, T14, D16 18, T20, B
129	T19, T16, D12 T19, T12, D18 T19, T20, D6 T19, D16, D20 T19, D18, D18 19, T20, B

130	T20, T20, D5 T20, 20, B
131	T20, T13, D16 T20, T17, D10 T17, D20, D20
132	B, B, D16 B, T14, D20 O/B, T19, B
133	T20, T19, D8 T19, D19, D19
134	T20, T14, D16 T20, T18, D10 T18, D20, D20
135	B, T15, D20 B, T19, D14 O/B, T20, B T19, T18, D12
136	T20, T20, D8
137	T20, T19, D10 T19, T16, D16 T19, D20, D20
138	T20, T18, D12 T19, T19, D12 T20, T20, D9
139	T20, T13, D20 T20, T19, D11 T19, B, D16

	T19, T14, D20
140	T20, T20, D10 T18, T18, D16 T20, D20, D20
141	T20, T19, D12 T20, T15, D18 T17, T18, D18
142	T20, B, D16 T20, T14, D20 T20, T20, D11 T17, T17, D20
143	T20, T17, D16 T19, T18, D16
144	T20, T20, D12 T18, T18, D18
145	T20, T15, D20 T20, T19, D14
146	T20, T18, D16 T19, T19, D16 T20, T20, D13
147	T20, T17, D18 T19, T18, D18 T19, B, D20
148	T20, T20, D14 T18, T18, D20 T20, T16, D20

149	T20, T19, D20
150	T20, T18, D18 T19, T19, D18 T20, T20, D15 T20, B, D20 B, B, B
151	T20, T17, D20 T19, T18, D20
152	T20, T20, D16
153	T20, T19, D18
154	T20, T18, D20 T19, T19, D20
155	T20, T19, D19
156	T20, T20, D18
157	T20, T19, D20
158	T20, T20, D19
159	No Finish
160	T20, T20, D20
161	T20, T17, B T19, T18, B
164	T20, T18, B T19, T19, B
167	T20, T19, B

170	T20, T20, B

Thank You!

Did you enjoy this book? You can make a big difference.

Reviews are the most powerful tools in my arsenal when it comes to getting attention for my books. Much as I'd like to, I don't have the financial muscle of a New York publisher. I can't take out full page ads in the newspaper or put posters on the subway.

But I do have something much more powerful and effective than that, and it's something that those publishers would kill to get their hands on.

A committed and loyal bunch of readers.

Honest reviews of my books help bring them to the attention of other readers.

If you've enjoyed this book, I would be very grateful if you could spend just five minutes leaving a review (it can be as short as you like). You can find the book on the platform where you purchased it.

Thank you very much.

About the Author

From very early on in his darting journey in England, Jim realized that even though he wasn't the best player around, he possessed a World Class knowledge of how to finish. He very quickly became the go-to guy wherever he went, helping other players with their finishes. Although he doesn't actively play anymore, Jim never lost his passion for the game. He realized that just about every Darts Player out there could benefit from the knowledge contained in this series of books, whatever their level of play. He posts and blogs at *http://dartsfinishing.com/*

Other Books in this series:

Darts Finishing Mastery - Advanced Strategies

This book is for those of you that have the desire, drive, and dedication to become exceptional...

You are already a player that continually strives to improve their game with regular, focused practice. You understand the importance of knowing all the finishing combinations from 2-170. But what about all the numbers above those? How far do you go before starting to think about the finish? The answer may come as a shock to you.

This book continues on from where **Darts Finishing Mastery - How to Master the Art of Finishing** ends. It concentrates on the vital Second Phase of the 501 game - the Set Up Phase. This is often the most overlooked, and yet one of the most important phases of 501. It literally can make the difference in-between being a good player and being a world beater. That is how important it is. And yet very few players take the time to study this vital aspect of the game.

It takes dedication and a lot of practice to be proficient at this level, but if you are aiming to be the very best you can be, you need to reserve a sizable part of your practice time to learn and master this area of your game. If you do, the rewards can be life changing.

If this describes you, then you are ready for Darts Finishing Mastery: Advanced Strategies…

Find it here:

<u>**Darts Finishing Mastery - Advanced Strategies**</u>

Other Books in this series:

All About the Bullseye

Nothing confuses a Darts Player more than the little round bit in the middle. When should you go for it? When should it be used as a part of a combination shot? What tactical advantages can it bring to the player? Does it work the same for every situation? All this, and more are answered in this very important book that should be in every Dart's Players Library.

This book is a part of a 4-book series that are designed to give any darts player a complete and thorough education in the art of Darts Finishing. If ever there was a university course in the Darts Finishing, this is what they would be teaching:

- Remove all the mystique surrounding the Bullseye once and for all
- Know with pinpoint precision when - and importantly - when not to use the Bullseye
- Knock years off your learning curve
- Know different, effective strategies for finishing, depending on the situation
- Gain a massive advantage over your opponents
- Develop unshakable confidence in your finishing
- All this and much, much more.

Find it here:

Darts Finishing Mastery - All About the Bullseye

Other Books in this series:

The 7 Pillars of Darts

There are 7 critical numbers that are so strategically important that there is a book dedicated to them. Every Darts Player should be aware of these "Pillar" numbers and utilize them in their finishing strategy.

Once learned, they will take your finishing to new heights, and give you a massive advantage over your opponents. If you are a player that has aspirations of reaching the business ends of tournaments on a regular basis, then this book is for you. This is a book that simply has to be in every Darts Player's library.

This book is a part of a 4-book series that are designed to give any darts player a complete and thorough education in the art of Darts Finishing. If ever there was a university course in the Darts Finishing, this is what they would be teaching:

- Learn the 7 most important numbers in finishing
- Know instinctively how-to set-up finishes from seemingly impossible positions
- Knock years off your learning curve
- Know different, effective strategies for finishing depending on the situation
- Gain a massive advantage over your opponents
- Master the dartboard
- All this and much, much more.

Find it here:

Darts Finishing Mastery - The 7 Pillars of Darts

Printed in Poland
by Amazon Fulfillment
Poland Sp. z o.o., Wrocław

30460814R00130